Addictive LIES

A SURVIVOR'S GUIDE TO ADDICTION

V.M. Lawrence, PhD

Addictive Lies: A Survivor's Guide to Addiction

Copyright © 2011 by V.M. Lawrence

Published by Carpenter's Son Publishing, Franklin, Tennessee

Published in association with Larry Carpenter of Christian Book Services, LLC
www.christianbookservices.com

Cover and Interior Layout Design: Suzanne Lawing

Printed in the United States of America

978-0-9839876-3-5

Table of Contents

Preface

Now that this book has been written, I will begin at the beginning. This may sound like a strange statement, but it is one which I have struggled with since the onset of *Addictive Lies*. Actually, the struggle began over forty years ago.

I will not attempt to justify my actions or place blame because there are many factors that contributed to my inherited and chosen lifestyles. Neither will I accept blame, for each of us has been given a cross to carry and addiction is mine. Having fallen under the weight of my cross many times, bruised and shaking, I finally allowed myself the freedom to share this burden with others.

Addiction is a burden, but who in life is without burden? My mother was fond of saying, "That which does not kill you makes you stronger." Agreed—providing we find the truth in our lives (the truth of whom and what we are)—for it is the truth that lessens the burden of the cross.

Addiction is a dubious blessing, for all burdens, despite the inflicting of pain, also provide opportunities for understanding and change—the very tools needed for life satisfaction.

Depending upon individual perception, we can concede defeat and wallow in self-pity or accept the burden of addiction and our inability to carry it alone. Like all things in life, ongoing addiction is a choice, not a lifelong curse.

Making choices presumes a need to change, which while not always easy, usually occurs after continued failure, until one glorious day, failure leads to success. But what is success? To addicts, success ends the private and social alienation that restricts normal everyday functioning. To addicts, success is the distinction between inbred lies and the acceptance of self-truth.

So then what is self-truth? It is truth determined by our Divine origin and life purpose. Our worth, pre-established by the Creator, cannot be altered by the faulty perceptions of others. It also cannot be devalued by individuals whose own self-worth has been compromised—and it cannot be determined by addiction.

Addiction is not a life purpose—certainly not mine—for it exists amid and beyond the disgust and condemnation of addicts to provide hope to those who have forgotten how to hope.

It is not my intention to inflict further pain, for we are all expert at self-punishment while sadly lacking at self-forgiveness and love.

Addiction is not a life sentence unless the behavior is allowed to continue; otherwise the sentence can be credited to time already served as we are remanded into our own custody.

Addictive Lies, while establishing commonalities among addictive behaviors, also provides workable suggestions to counter these learned behaviors. Yes, I believe that addiction is learned. And what has been learned can be replaced by positive and healthy behaviors.

Addictive Lies was written for those desiring to reclaim life on their own terms and without limitation to soar on the powerful wings of God-given potential. It is our right. And all we need to do is reach out to claim it.

If you can't control the wind, adjust the sail.

Addictive Lies seems to divide naturally into three sections, including introduction and background information, fifteen practical suggestions for the addict, and related subjects. It was my intention to provide a helpful guide for those struggling to reclaim a purposeful existence based on self-love and respect.

Questions for discussion:

What is your definition of an addict?

Does this definition fit you or anyone you know?

How does this make you feel?

Are you willing to do anything about it?

Part One
Chapter 1

* * *

Addictive Lies
(Surviving Addiction)

People, like all of God's creations, must find balance in existence. If a plant is improperly nourished, if it does not receive adequate amounts of water, air, and nutrients, it withers and dies. Similarly, if any or all human components—mind, body, and spirit (heart)—are neglected, we will feel, think, and act in a manner contradictory to our inner being because we are out of balance.

But, unlike plants, we are able to control our environment. If we sense dissatisfaction, there is a multitude of activities available to relieve boredom or spark interest. Whatever it takes, we are amazingly adaptive at restoring life-satisfaction. We crave balance, that feeling of well-being, and the inner harmony that states all is right in our world.

We interpret and react to life events according to past experiences or learned behavior. These learned behaviors have the flexibility to fit into situations containing similarities and enable us to automatically react without having to constantly define the responsive behavior.

Restoration of balance and learned reaction to situations possessing commonalities provide the basis for potential addictive behavior. In other words, we all want to feel good and tend to repeat what makes us feel good.

* * *

Mind, body, and heart interact to maintain or restore the interior balance essential to our sense of well-being. It is in this generalized state that attitude and behavior are determined as each of the three components attempt to satisfy or justify their individualistic needs.

Striving to feel good—mind, body, and heart will either naturally complement each other or one will override the others— leads to artificially compensating for what is perceived to be lacking in order to attain balance. The goal is the feel-good 'high' resulting naturally through harmonious, loving, and respectful interaction or the incorporation of artificial means like self-medication, defined as addictive substances. Whatever means are employed, the motivational factor is always the same—to create a sense of well-being or balance among mind, body, and heart.

Balanced Heart (joy-filled)	Unbalanced Heart (empty)

Mind (accepting)	Body (healthy)	Mind (controlling)	Body (abused)

* * *

We are largely influenced by our experiences. Our reality is based upon the perception of these experiences, not upon the experiences themselves. The way life events are perceived is more powerful because our minds uniquely interpret everything that affects our being. It is this interpretation that determines the good or bad of a situation and establishes a foundation upon which to interpret similar future events. It is also this perception that either inhibits or encourages life exploration and change. Perception of past events determines our present and future.

Many lives are stuck in the past due to faulty perception. Many people are stunted in growth due to unreasonable expectations. And many lives suffer the memory of the daily put-downs of the 'not enoughs'—not being good enough or smart enough or pretty enough or thin enough, etc. This results in unresolved pain worn like a cloak to disguise a deteriorating essence—keeping us from that which makes us uniquely us, with all our God-given talents and limitations, or God within us.

Excitedly waiting for the class to begin, I stood at the barre while the miniature ballerinas, all dressed identically in black leotards, pink tights, and slippers, engaged in animated conversation. Feeling conspicuously out of place in denim shorts, a white T-shirt, and socks, I was certain they were all talking about me.

The sight of Madame caught my breath, for she was the most beautiful creature I had ever seen as she glided swan-like across the polished floor. Her presence hushed the room. She scrutinized the miniatures with nodding approval and then, with a deep sigh, ventured forward to meet the newest class member.

I did my best to follow, and toward the end of the class, Madame requested that we pirouette across the room. This I could do, for I did it at home millions of times.

Confident in my ability, I began the gliding twirl of a prima ballerina. Effortlessly, my arms and legs carried me around and around—and I knew that at last, I was one of them—one of the miniatures.

After class, I noticed Madame speaking with my mother, so I ran to bask in the compliments no doubt being rained upon my performance!

"You would do best," Madame said, "not to further waste your money. Unfortunately, your daughter has absolutely no talent for dance. I am sorry."

Piano lessons began the following week—a pursuit for which the music teacher assured mother that I did have talent. (I hated the piano—I wanted to dance.)

Faulty perceptions—the 'not-beings' resulting from misinformation provided by others—establish negativity, and negativity breeds negativity. It is detrimental to our well-being for it separates us from God's positive, life-affirming truth.

And what is God's truth? We possess worth since we are created in His image. God is love and since He is love, we through inheritance, are loveable—each in our own unique way. We are worthy of giving and receiving love regardless of our talents and limitations. God's truth is the inner strength that we lack.

Addictive behavior prevents the giving and receiving of love (to self and others) because it separates us from God by denying our God-given worth. It is the consolation prize for the 'not beings'—a balancing act without the use of a harness or net, disguising reality with fantasy.

* * *

We all want fulfillment and joy in our lives. We want to feel healthy and energetic. We want peace—and we don't want pain. We also don't want haunting memories or negativity to control our thoughts and behavior. We want to live in a state of well-being, whether naturally or artificially induced. We want life-satisfaction, not dissatisfaction.

We want to be loved.

I don't remember ever being in my father's tender embrace and hearing those three beautiful and life-essential words, "I love you."

* * *

In natural balance, based on a loving, trusting relationship with God, we accept our human limitations and dependency on One greater than ourselves. It is a free-will decision involving intellect and heart, which instead of reducing us to a childlike state, empowers us with the strength of His love.

I am at my strongest and best when actively in the present—for God is in the present. Since the past is memory and the future is still distant, all we actually have is the present. Uninhibited by memories and fears (imaginings of what might occur, which are non-reality based), the present exists to link us with God, for living in the present means living in the presence of God.

Life-dissatisfaction—that omnipresent feeling that something is missing or wrong, regardless of accomplishments—indicates an interior void. This gnawing presence that usurps the everyday joy of living is the driving factor for restorative balance.

Artificial balance is self-created. It is a God-less balance that offers cover-ups—solutions that are transient and shallow, providing immediate surface satisfaction without consideration of deeper needs. It is a quick fix that temporarily feels good, employing 'things' to achieve balance without maintenance.

When God is neglected or rejected, a God-less void forms in the heart causing unrest and disrupting balance. And since balance must be maintained, mind and body will always seek "things" to fill the heart-void.

But, God is the only lasting filler, so the means found or restorative efforts made by mind and body are only short-lived imitations; imposters promising instant satisfaction; lesser gods assuming magnified importance with persuasive qualities attractive to the mind and body. They lure with shiny promises of satisfaction and relief from the empty restlessness created by the heart-void, but it is like applying a Band-Aid to a deep wound when a tourniquet is required. Society's lesser gods, mass-created assumptions concerning human satisfaction, are born of ignorance and greed.

Doomed to failure, additional solutions are needed—and when these fail too, more will be necessary—always more, for these lesser gods are costly and very demanding.

"Learn then that I, I alone, am God,

and there is no god besides me." (Deuteronomy 32: 39)

Nothing else will truly satisfy. No One else can fill the heart-void.

Although a relationship with God is priceless, His monetary cost is nothing. He requires our presence and love. His unconditional love is not fickle. It is a gracious lasting love that is capable of completely and permanently filling the heart-void.

But He is a demanding God, for He states, "Whoever does not carry his cross and come after me cannot be my disciple" (Luke 15:27).

But no matter the situation in which we find ourselves, the saving presence of God is with us- we are not alone. We do not have to be worthy or carry our cross alone, for He is waiting for us to turn to Him in what may seem to be the darkest darkness..."lo, I am with you always...(Mathew 28:20). The protecting presence of God is all around us. "Though I walk in the midst of trouble, thou hast preserved my life... and thy right hand delivers me (Psalms 138:7). We are never alone.

It is life that has value and the quality of the life that determines the value. Since all life comes from God, all life has value. We are born equal, yet what accounts for expressions of laughter and joy on some faces while others register despair? What accounts for the sense of worth in some lives and the worthlessness in others? What accounts for addictive behavior?

* * *

The voice of the heart is often unheard for it is a mere whisper in a world demanding our attention. Like a shy child, it stands back hoping to be noticed while other noisy children vie for attention. An interior quiet that longs to be recognized and longs for fulfillment—the heart suffers the loneliness of the misunderstood.

There is no substitute for love. No amount of control or materialism or human excess can fill a heart-void. Only love.

God's heart is that no one should ever be victimized by abusive substances (anything used in excess to fill the heart-void that negatively impacts balance and well-being, and separates us from God). God wants no one to shoulder the guilt and shame associated with addiction—nor harbor a history of pain and suffering. It was never God's heart that people would become addicts.

* * *

God is the key to overcoming any addiction. He is the key that unlocks the freedom of truth. He is the Physician of last resort when other futile attempts have failed. He is the Scale that balances mind, body, and heart. He is the Truth that saves.

Truth releases the bonds of addiction. God's truth (grace) restores balance and well-being by filling the heart-void.

As addicts, we must seek the truth about ourselves while relying upon His strength for our cure. We have tried and we CAN NOT cure ourselves—we can no longer do it alone. For...

"Mortals are a mere breath,
the powerful but an illusion;
On a balance they rise;
together they are lighter than air." (Psalms 62:10)

Since I don't believe in formalized declarations of addiction, the following section, while difficult, is necessary to validate Addictive Lies, which is based on personal and professional experience.

As a child, I was taught to keep "the family's dirty laundry to ourselves." To state that I am an alcoholic (this revelation, although by no means a secret, is difficult to see on the written page) is far from the truth for I am so much more. I am a teacher and healer. I am a writer, a mother, a sister, a friend. I am loving and I am compassionate.

And like everyone else, I have a cross to bear. My particular cross is alcoholism.

I was raised in a contradiction of realities between family and Church. Saturday morning I went to religious instruction. Saturday afternoon, we (my mother and I) confessed our sins. On Sunday morning we attended mass. (My father, being somehow exempt, stated that we, not he, were in need of such practices.)

God is love. God is peace. But this God existed only within the walls of St. Catherine's, for at home, Satan reigned with tongues of anger and belittlement. Fear, not peace nor love, controlled my life—creating a contradiction between the church teachings and my everyday reality.

Harsh words and flared tempers were my everyday reality— a reality that turned me away from God, for how could He profess His love while allowing me, a vulnerable child, to endure the wrath of two embittered parents?

Addiction is a psychological dependency, a learned behavior. It is not physical, it is emotional. It is not a disease, but a terminal wound that we attempt to salve alone. It is an escape route in times of weakness. A predetermined vacation destination when the world closes in and we fear loss of control.

In life, diseases such as cancer occur with or without our consent. Cancer is not a life choice, but an unfortunate physical abnormality.

Addiction is a choice and therefore not a disease. Before we pick up a needle or reach for a bottle, we have a choice. (The defining word here is before. After, the choice becomes mute.)

I met a man in Erie, PA who told me this story about his aunt who at age 66 suffered a stroke. She was an alcoholic who reportedly consumed more than a liter of vodka daily. Her recovery went well except for a slight memory loss.

It was at a family gathering that people noticed and began talking for she appeared sober and was not drinking. As the party progressed her relatives, who could no longer ignore this strange behavior, asked if she would like a drink.

Her response was, "No thank you. I don't drink." She simply forgot her reliance on alcohol and, due to memory loss, she had no addictive behavioral recall or craving, vowing that she "never touched the stuff." (Obviously, additional research is necessary, but isn't this interesting?)

Addiction is a psychological dependency, a learned behavior. And memory keeps the behavior active.

Addiction is also the result of faulty coping skills.

As a child, I had ineffective coping skills, so I turned within, like a turtle seeking the protection of its shell. I couldn't talk about "our dirty laundry."(My grandparents, who lived less than twenty minutes away, never knew. Yet, the neighbors knew, for they heard it all.)

Once I courageously asked my mother why she and father were always angry. Within seconds I became the recipient of that anger. So, I learned to remain quiet and withdraw my head in the silence of anonymity as an invisible child.

My first drink was taken at age thirteen. Divulging additional details is unnecessary. But, what is necessary is to state that self-worth is not determined by others—for our worth was pre-determined prior to existence. And contrary belief is but acceptance of lies disguised as the truth.

I handled pain and disappointment by reverting back to the stunted skills of that hurting child. Withdrawing within, I become that invisible child again and again, accepting each setback as personal rejection because I was just not good enough or smart enough to succeed and be loved.

Today I am no longer that vulnerable, frightened child of my youth, and withdrawal— the numbness of feeling—is no longer acceptable.

Questions for discussion:

What makes you feel good?

Does your heart feel empty? Explain.

Do you attempt to control life? Explain.

Or does your life feel out of control?

Room for Thoughts

_____

_____

_____

_____

_____

_____

_____

_____

_____

_____

_____

_____

_____

_____

_____

_____

_____

_____

_____

_____

_____

_____

_____

Chapter 2

* * *

Addiction

Addiction is a continuing ill-fated attempt to regain balance through excessive external means. It is a dependency of choice intended to mask, not alleviate, internal pain. We are not born addicts. We become addicts when functional living becomes too difficult. Addiction is escape from perceived reality, a reality that haunts and tortures mind, body, and heart without reprieve.

Addiction is extreme behavior evoked to neutralize extreme emotions. It is a lonely and selfish pursuit that serves to isolate the addict from purposeful living, from others, and from God.

Addition is the physical manifestation of the emotional state we crave—pleasure and the release from pain. Addictive substances provide emotional highs on cue—no waiting, just instantaneous pleasure.

Little is accomplished by public proclamation. Some programs require addicts to stand before other sufferers and state their abusive behavior. This practice is both humiliating and serves limited purpose, for addiction is not a well-kept secret. Although self-contained, it is hardly a private affair. Pain causes addiction, so why inflict further pain and humiliation upon the sufferer? Why add to the existing guilt and shame that required self-medication in the first place? It's like rubbing the addict's face in his dirty diaper—it accomplishes nothing.

I've witnessed individuals bolstering their courage just outside the doors of addiction meetings with one last gulp from the bottle. And I've witnessed those leaving the meetings to regroup at the nearest bar.

The first meeting I attended had a similar effect. I hesitated before entering, feeling extremely self-conscious and conspicuous. My mind screamed that I didn't belong, that I had nothing in common. But, I did—no denial here. I am an addict.

What bothered me, what I couldn't relate to, was the lack of movement in their lives. They seemed to exist for the meetings, proudly rattling off the number attended that week. I don't want to count the number of meetings I've attended.

I want so much more out of life. I don't want to wallow in past transgressions, stating and restating my history of addiction. I simply want my life back. I want to live.

There is no need to apologize for addiction. Forgiveness is required, not apology.

Addiction is a serious error in judgment and a corruption of the will. In an effort to regain balance, the addict, through ignorance, rejection, or neglect, replaces the Divine with the lesser "gods" found in bottles, needles, and checkbooks that offer pleasure at an ever-increasing price; gods that dull the truth by promising quick fixes and instant gratification.

We all have our "little addictions"—another pair of shoes stuffed into already bulging closets or that secret stash of dark chocolate nestled behind the cereal boxes in the back of the pantry. They are life's little "got-to-haves" calling you by name.

Society determines acceptable amounts and frequency of addictive substances. For example, social drinking is acceptable—everyday drunkenness is not. Eating is pleasurable—emotional eating resulting in obesity is not.

Visibility is another factor in addiction. Since society is critical of nonconforming behavior, deviants are judged harshly under watchful eyes. The excessiveness of addiction is highly visible and, although to the addict, addiction remains a private affair, once societal norms are breeched, judgment swiftly ensues.

The need for an occasional escape from the concerns and humdrum of everydayness does not presume addiction, for these temporary retreats are made in full expectation of returning reality. We all splurge occasionally. Addiction is not an occasional splurge.

Addiction is a total life-escape—the means to end the nonstop suffering. And oblivion appears to be the answer—oblivion from the world and from ourselves.

Addiction removes free will, the power enabling us to make choices. The addict's will has been usurped, corrupted, and bent to the will of the "lesser gods" who hold it captive without ransom.

Addiction is a shame-filled pursuit. When individuals cross the socially established line of demarcation, they are labeled "addicts"—a term only fully understood by other addicts. For society, labeling is easier than understanding, but it only serves to heap additional shame upon the addict's already sagging shoulders—creating further need for escape.

* * *

Growing up, we receive flawed information based on the flawed and biased assessments of others. Through words and actions, or the withholding of words and actions, we learn who and what we are. We learn self-worth, our strengths, and our limitations based on the perceptions of others. Whether intentional or unintentional, these perceptions are the initial determinants for our life-potential.

If the information is exaggerated with an unrealistic assessment of our abilities, feelings of guilt and shame occur due to the impossibility of achieving the expected. If expectations are too low, achievement will be low, for we tend to live up to others' perceptions. Whether expectations are too high or too low, we are paralyzed by the "L" branded on our foreheads and in our minds. If the loser symbol 'L' is not erased by self-discovery, we remain emotionally stunted by the faulty perceptions of others.

* * *

Childhood affirmation (consistency of loving care and treatment) is required to build trust. If positive reinforcement is lacking or inconsistent, the ability to fully trust in our own goodness and self-worth is diminished. Inconsistent or negative affirmation prevents us from trusting others and the world becomes a lonely and scary place.

As a child, I would hold my breath before entering the house and count to ten. Afraid, yet realizing that I had no place else to go, I hoped for the best—never knowing what to expect when I opened the door. I would stop and listen...and then proceed with caution.

In order to grow and achieve full potential, we must take chances. Only by exposing ourselves to the opportunities imbedded in new situations can growth and development occur. Trust allows this to happen. Distrust confines us to stagnation.

Addiction is the end result of faulty assessment, labeling limitations, the guilt and shame associated with the worthlessness of the "not enoughs," the frustration of stagnation that disallows growth, and of dormant qualities never to be realized. Addiction is the end result of simply giving up.

Addictive lies, whether rooted in "other-frustration" or "other-envy," affect self-esteem and self-worth—negatively impacting thought and limiting behavior. Addictive lies affect the level of self- and other-trust, as well as love, which detrimentally impacts relationships. For if we can't love and trust ourselves, how can we love and trust another?

Once this message of failure is internalized, life becomes a series of self-fulfilling prophesies as we set out to justify our worthlessness. This is what we believe—we fail because we are failures. And as failures, we are destined to fail.

Addiction is an endless cycle of self-abuse based on hurtful, addictive lies in an attempt to restore balance and end the pain of "the not beings."

The Knots Prayer
Dear God:
Please untie the knots that are in my mind,
my heart, and my life.
Remove the have nots, the can nots, and the
do nots that I have in my mind.
Erase the will nots, may nots that may find a
home in my heart.
Release me from the could nots, would nots,
and should nots that obstruct my life.
And most of all, Dear God,
I ask that you remove from my mind, my heart,
And my life all of the 'am nots' that I have allowed
to hold me back. —Author known only to God

Discovery of the truth will counteract the lies masking our identity. Only the truth will restore mind, body, and heart balance. The addict, in order to survive, must discover that truth (God-given truth, not others-given lies), for it is God's truth that frees us from pain and guilt and addiction.

Questions for discussion:
How do you react to addicts? Can you identify with them?

Are certain types of addiction more or less ok? Explain.

Do you suffer from the "not-enough"s?

How do you cope with disappointment? Explain and rate your coping skills.

As a child, did you receive positive or negative affirmation?

Are you open to new opportunities? Can you take chances? Or do you prefer to maintain that which is known and comfortable?

What do others expect from you? What do you expect from yourself? Have you attained these expectations? Why or why not?

Room for Thoughts

Chapter 3

* * *

Pride

Human beings are prideful creatures. With the birth of pride (original sin), man fell from God's grace. Although the capacity for achieving oneness was restored (through Christ's death and resurrection), pride remains a barrier. False pride boasts self-salvation and control while accepting credit for God-given gifts and abilities. We tend to take credit for our successes and blame others (including God) for our failures. Because of our fallen nature, we tend to be led only by what satisfies us. It is both our inheritance and our downfall because pride blinds us from the truth. "Pride goes before disaster and a haughty spirit before a fall" (Proverbs 16:18).

Pride prevents us from admitting our weaknesses and limitations. It prevents us from acknowledging dependency on the One greater than ourselves. It provides excuses and blame for failure.

Pride also prevents us from seeking help, for it is an admission that we are not in control, and that we are floundering in circumstances beyond our capacity. Pride is irrational, boastful, human vanity accepting credit for intellect and ability which in reality are God-given gifts.

This frequently used word, *pride*, translates into hurt feelings when life doesn't behave as expected (i.e., "My pride is hurt"). Pride results in an affront to our sense of entitlement and self-centered control.

We cannot control situations or people. The only control we possess is over ourselves in our words and actions. This is a concept difficult to accept due to the resistance of human pride.

We need to acknowledge and accept who actually is in control of life—it is not us.

Pride, like blinders on a race horse, often limits visionary thought and action by creating tunnel-view options while ignoring a broader world spectrum. Pride can be harmful when it supersedes common sense in dealing with self and others. "Man's pride causes his humiliation..." (Proverbs 29:23).

Losing one's pride is hurtful. Having pride usurped without consent is painful. But when consent is given, and when pride is surrendered in humility and love, that constitutes freedom. The relinquishment of imaginary control releases the burden of life's responsibility while returning control to its rightful owner—and that is life-altering.

> "You must give up your old way of life: you must put aside your old self, which gets corrupted by illusory desires. Your minds must be renewed by a spiritual revolution so that you can put on the new self that has been created in God's way, in the goodness and holiness of the truth" (Ephesians 4:22).

I recently heard an acronym for ego—edging God out. Now isn't that what a pride-filled ego does?

We are a pride-filled people and it is only when the pride is knocked out of us that we find humility. And humility is humbling.

Questions for discussion:

What are your weaknesses/limitations?

Are you controlling? Do you blame others? Give examples.

Are you pride-filled? Give examples of behavior.

Do you consider yourself a success or failure? Explain.

Room for Thoughts

Chapter 4

* * *

Self-Worth

We are created by the Divine. So, if God is love, we must at our essence be love. If God is strength and beauty, we are strength and beauty. If we mirror His likeness, we are goodness and forgiving.

> "God created man in His image,
>   in the divine image He created him;
>   male and female He created them" (Genesis 1: 27).

But, we only mirror God. We are not, nor were we ever intended to be, gods. We are not self-saviors. That is why in our human weakness we must seek Him with an open and trusting heart. As His creation, He cares for us. "See! I will not forget you…I have carved you on the palm of My hand" (Isaiah 49:15).

In today's world, it is easy to be devalued by the faulty judgment of addictive lies, or celebrated for successes and possessions. These are not indicators of value, but measures of human superficiality. True value lies in our roots (who we are) and we are all rooted in the Divine.

> "He made from one (blood) the whole human race…
>   so that people might seek God, even perhaps grope for Him and
>   find Him, though indeed He is not far from any one of us.
>   For 'In Him we live and move and have our being'…we are
>   His offspring" (Acts 17: 26-28).

As God's offspring, we are so much more than can ever be imagined. Or, as is so beautifully stated by Marianne Williamson in *In A Return to Love*, "Our deepest fear is not that we are inadequate. Our deepest fear is that we are powerful beyond measure. It is our light, not our darkness, that most frightens us. We ask ourselves, who am I to be brilliant, gorgeous, talented, or fabulous? Actually, who are you not to be? You are a child of God."

As children of God, our worth is beyond measure, yet we are so easily persuaded and convinced otherwise. If the truth lies in our hearts, why do we not know this truth? The answer is simple: we have disconnected from our hearts—from our God-source.

Who am I? What is life's purpose? These are questions for conjecture spanning generations since the onset of humanity. We think about and discuss the meaning of life—employing our limited knowledge and resources. We intellectualize or just speculate, often pleased with the sound of our own voices.

Yet who knows you better than the Creator who formed you from nothing; the Sublime Being who knew your thoughts and words before you even existed; He who loved you since the beginning of time and who will love you for eternity?

Since God-truth resides within the heart (the essence and core of our being), we must look there for the answers concerning our life purpose and call, which was decided long ago by Divine will. We must also remove all personal barriers and all distractions that divert our energy from discovery.

Society tends to compromise our need-dependency upon the Divine Connection with its "survival of the fittest" mentality. As in the animal world, society teaches strength and cunning as laws of self-preservation. And we stand alone, facing the world alone, believing in the sanctity of our aloneness with disregard for the omnipresence of the Almighty.

> "If I flew to the point of the sunrise,
>   or westward across the sea,
>   your hand will still be guiding me,
>   your right hand holding me" (Psalms 139:8-10).

The good news is that we are not alone. From humdrum everydayness to life's momentous decisions, we are never alone. During joy and darkness, we are not alone.

Regardless of perceived power or societal status, the bottom line is, we are one with God and love—equals in His eyes. Uniquely talented, we are all called to a unique purpose predetermined by the same Creator. Our only choice is whether or not to accept the invitation.

A true assessment of self-worth blends God-origin with human failings. We seem to gravitate toward the worldly preoccupations which disguise, but do not diminish, our greater value. It is this hidden value that needs to be acknowledged with consideration of our weaknesses in order to allow acceptance of the invitation.

A yes response indicates acknowledgment of dependency on a Higher Source, a realization that personal control is illusionary and beyond human ability, and the understanding of a heart-need that worldly offerings cannot supply. "Yes" means submission to God's will with hope-filled trust that all will be well. With this conviction, our now God-centered life takes on a new purpose—His purpose, which is the purpose that He intended before our existence. So, answer the invitation and RSVP your "yes."

We all have value, although for many, that value is as clouded as ill-prescribed glasses perched on our noses. We can't see clearly, but the phone number of an extremely competent optometrist is within hand's reach.

Along with lost glasses, the addict has also lost the phone number. There seems to be no recourse, no reprieve from years of self- and other heart-inflicted abuse. Stripped of worth and purpose, the invitation was returned due to insufficient postage.

A Prayer of Healing
Lord Jesus, you came to heal our wounded and troubled hearts,
I beg you to heal the torments that cause anxiety in my heart;
I beg you to heal all which are the cause of sin.
I beg you to come into my life and heal me of the psychological harms that
    struck me in my early years
and from the injuries that they have caused throughout my life.
Lord you know my burdens…I lay them on Your Heart.
Heal the pain of my memories, so that nothing that has happened to me
    will cause me to remain in pain and anguish, filled with anxiety.

Heal, O Lord, all those wounds that have been the cause of all the evil
    that is rooted in my life.
I want to forgive all those who have offended me.
Look to those inner sores that have made me unable to forgive…
    (and) please, heal my own heart.

Heal those intimate wounds that cause me physical illness.
I offer you my heart, accept it Lord… —Fr. Gabriel Amoth

Man's heart is so delicate and complex that only through knowing God can it know itself.

Questions for discussion:

What are your addictive lies? Are they true or untrue?

Who are you? Are you fabulous?

What is your true value? Assess your self-worth.

What are your unique talents? What makes you uniquely you?

What is your unique life purpose?

Look within your heart. What is it telling you?

What is your truth?

Room for Thoughts

Chapter 5

* * *

Trust

Whom do you trust? Do you trust yourself? Others? God?

Trust is learned during childhood through the reception of loving and affirming behavior initiated by caregivers. The consistency of affirmation enables trust and reinforces our sense of lovability and individual value. We know what to expect and trust in the fulfillment of that expectation. We learn to trust in the goodness and consistency of ourselves and others.

Reception of inconsistent or negative behavior diminishes our ability to trust. As recipients of unwarranted belittlement resulting from others' anger and frustration, the world becomes fearful (punishing) and others become untrustworthy (hurtful). Individual potential is stunted as opportunities are dismissed along with the desire to change (growth).

With trust there is hope, for hope is the byproduct of learned trust—hope-filled in the expectation that goodness and acceptance will prevail. Without trust, there is no hope—only the hopelessness of continuing disappointment and the expectation of lovelessness. Without hope, there is despair. Without self-love, there can be no God-love.

Negative self-worth is internalized to the exclusion of others in an "I-don't-need-anyone" attitude. Others are shunned as we see suspect motives in them and we display the pretense of self-sufficiency, while the constant need for acceptance by others is denied.

I have raised three children alone without financial or physical assistance. This I consciously chose to do for I trusted no one. My marriage and ensuing relationships were all doomed due to the lack of trust—for I was self-sufficient and needed no one.

This faulty self-trust can evolve into a mechanism of self-preserving willfulness (self-centered for others-centered is not possible). Yet as a pretense for real self-trust, it is lacking—a cover-up to protect and disguise the small child cringing beneath the bedcovers; the child fighting for survival while drowning in despair.

I liked having my own way with no one around to disagree—even though willfulness is a very lonely pursuit.

Willfulness is controlling, it is illusionary. For although we believe we are in control, in reality we can control nothing but ourselves. As a defense mechanism for the shame of the "not enoughs," willfulness is designed to keep others at arm's length.

I have dated and rejected many individuals, for it is better to reject than be rejected. Along the way I have also rejected any possibility of love.

Willfulness is protection against the fear of closeness. It is a loveless state, for love cannot exist where there is fear.

Willfulness erects walls to shield against the hurtful lies perceived as truth. It blinds us to possibilities—the give-and-take interactions founded in mutual respect. It is the first to hurt in order to prevent being hurt.

Willfulness is exhausting, yet we resist letting go even though we realize through constant mistakes and discontent that we are NOT in charge. We hang on, fearful of releasing that which does not exist—for there are no other anchors. Our trust is weak and weakness produces fear. And fear deflates trust.

Addicts are willful.

We cannot conquer others until we learn to conquer ourselves.

Conquest implies some degree of planned control. It implies motivation with an expected outcome. We can conquer (positive—victorious) or be conquered (negative—subservient). To be conquered indicates suppression or servitude—while to conquer means freedom.

Life is based on choices—the freedom to make choices. If this freedom is interfered with or somehow restrained, an objection is made. Yet in the battle of addiction, the white flag of surrender is waved from the onset—for the battle is rigged and the outcome predetermined. Like the story of David and Goliath, pitting two unevenly matched opponents against each other, only with one difference—David does not win.

It wasn't much of a fight. Ticket holders would surely demand a refund because

David never even picked up a rock. He never placed it in his slingshot or swung it over his head to hurl it at the mighty giant. David did nothing—but taste liquor for the first time or visit a pornographic website. Or perhaps he placed a bet at the racetrack or casino—innocuous behaviors for many individuals. But not for David, because relief was as welcoming as the arms of a lover.

The two opponents were unevenly matched. Mighty Goliath understood weakness and fed into David's innate need for balance between mind, body, and heart. He supplied David with newfound self-esteem and worth. He whispered words of eternal commitment to become David's constant companion, best friend, and lover.

I returned from a friend's house to ask mother if this friend could join us later that afternoon to go shopping. In a sudden fit of rage, mother grabbed my tongue in one hand and a sharp knife in the other and threatened to cut out my tongue if I ever again divulged our personal plans. Is it any wonder that trust became an issue?

The timid God-voice, innate in all humans, was extinguished like a candle in the wind because addictive relationships provide the consistent, affirmative behavior needed. As a substitute caregiver, addiction becomes the object of trust—developing into dependency and usurping the parental role by providing unconditional love and acceptance. Addiction has no expectations and never instills the guilt of the "not enoughs."

Like a puppet, the addict's strings are manipulated, binding him ever closer to addiction.

Nothing in life is certain or guaranteed, with one exception—God's love for us. On this we can always depend. He never abandons us and He never leaves us orphaned—we leave Him.

My will is to drink. God's will is for me NOT to drink.

"One night a man dreamed he was walking along the beach with the Lord. As scenes of his life flashed before him, he noticed that there were two sets of footprints in the sand. He also noticed at his saddest, lowest times there was but one set of footprints.

"This bothered the man. He asked the Lord, 'Did You not promise that if I gave my heart to You that You'd be with me all the way? Then why is there but one set of footprints during my most troublesome times?

"The Lord replied, 'My precious child, I love you and I would never forsake you. During those times of trial and suffering, when you see only one set of footprints, it was then I carried you." —Unknown author

"How great is your goodness, Lord…
You display it for those who trust in You" (Psalms 31: 20).

Questions for discussion:

Are you lovable? Explain. Do you love yourself? Why or why not?

Are you willful? Give examples.

Are you fear-filled? Give examples.

Whom do you trust? Yourself? Others? God? Why or why not?

Room for Thoughts

Chapter 6

* * *

Hope

Hope is an extension of trust. Without hope, life holds no surprises, no intriguing possibilities of what the day might bring nor pleasures that our minds have yet to conceive. Without hope, nothing exists to carry us through days of humdrum nothingness—and through days of pain and disappointment.

Hope is the reason to rise from bed in the morning and to return peacefully at day's end—knowing that the new dawn brings another day another day of hope when anything is possible.

People and events enter into our lives to affect change, bringing messages of hope and love if we are open to the communication and to the surprises they bring. If we are open with hope-filled expectations, we are never disappointed. But, if our minds and hearts are closed, God's everyday surprises and the joy of living are lost.

Hope is knowing that when the door imprinted with your name slams in your face, there will be another door opening—and another chance.

> "Be strong and take heart,
>   all you who hope in the Lord" (Psalms 31:25).

We concoct "pleasant schemes"—daydreams involving the "what ifs" in life or "wouldn't it be nice if...?" Self-indulgent amusements that, although they are hope-filled and self-willed, are not God-willed. They are usually choreographed according to our interpretation of how life should proceed, but life rarely goes according to our plan. It is only when self-will is removed from human schemes that God intervenes with more than we could possibly have hoped for—when God-will becomes our will.

How do we distinguish between self-will and God-will? The answer, when considered, is obvious—when the word 'I' is removed from thought it becomes God's will. Possession of the 'I' mentality recreates our selves as God's equal, placing humanity on par with the Divine. Try for just ten minutes to eliminate the 'I' from conversation and thought. It's difficult. This degree of difficulty shows the reliance and the importance we place upon ourselves in everyday life.

Like an obstacle course or a computer-generated game, life is wrought with the unexpected. Such as the sudden appearance of roadblocks that interrupt our way or detours that redirect or totally erase our decided following-path.

These roadblocks or speed bumps can be viewed negatively, immobilizing and frustrating future efforts. Or, they can be seen for what they are—hope-filled opportunities for change and growth. The viewing is personal choice.

Rich, potential-filled opportunities provide life-possibilities—the "what can be's" in life. Representing life's untapped blessings, they are there for the taking, if we open ourselves in hope to the wonders of God's love.

It's all right if a boulder blocks our following-path, for its placement wasn't accidental. Nothing in life is accidental, everything has purpose, including that boulder. If we take one step closer and then another, we might discover its life-altering purpose and the intention for its placement. And if we trust God's goodness, all is and will be well. That is hope.

Have you ever looked into a dark, angry sky, boiling with ominous clouds? Everything is obscured in shades of gray and black and then you notice one ray of light or one small patch of blue—that's hope.

We trust in God with hope-filled expectation.
"For in God our hearts rejoice;
in Your name we trust.
May Your kindness Lord be upon us;
we have put our hope in You" (Psalms 33:21-22).

Do not be afraid, for fear destroys hope. There is no room for fear in the heart in which God dwells, for fear cannot exist where there is love.

Saint Theresa's Prayer
May today there be peace within.
May you trust God that you are exactly where you were meant to be.
May you not forget the infinite possibilities that are born of faith.
May you use those gifts that you have received,

and pass on the love that has been given to you.

May you be confident knowing you are a child of God. Let this presence settle into your bones, and allow your soul the freedom to sing, dance, praise, and love.

It is there for each and every one of us.

Life isn't about waiting for the storm to pass. It's about learning to dance in the rain.
—Unknown author

Questions for discussion:

Define hope. Are you hope-filled? Give examples.

What are your hope-filled possibilities? Or is hope reserved for others?

Do you indulge in the "wouldn't-it-be-nice" game? Give an example.

Do you see roadblocks in your path or opportunities for change and growth?

Room for Thoughts

Chapter 7

* * *

God's Role in All This

Since we are created in God's image, we have the potential for attaining perfection, for He has thrown down the gauntlet, an invitation to strive to become more like Him. But, we can only strive for perfection, because if humanity was perfect, we would be gods and have no need of the Divine. And with Godlike power and wisdom, we could will perfection and happiness into our lives. A wonderful thought, but obviously just a fantasy.

As humans, we are fragile and fickle in emotion. We are weak of mind and heart. Our loyalties divide easily, lacking the constancy of unconditional love. We are flawed and the only redemptive feature of our flawed condition is our ability to acknowledge our limitations and reach out in humble trust to the Flawless One.

He provides the anchor when the winds of life threaten to capsize our boat. He is the One to whom we look for strength and guidance.

He is forgiveness and unconditional love. He forgives even when we cannot. He loves when we are unable to love ourselves.

He is our Creator and our Father. He knew us before our existence. He knew our words before they were spoken and our thoughts before they were conceived. He knows every molecule of our being. "The word is not even on my tongue, Yahweh, before You know all about it" (Psalms 139:4).

He knows our weaknesses and limitations. He knows our strengths and abilities. He knows our timidity of heart.

Who better to turn to than the One who knows us so intimately? He who knows us and still loves us? "He does not faint or grow weary, and His knowledge is beyond scrutiny" (Isaiah 40:28).

Who better to turn to when the world becomes unbearable? When life becomes too painful? "He gives strength to the fainting; for the weak he made vigor abound" (Isaiah 40:29).

The name of God, spoken in love and tenderness, drives away evil. It is the one word before which all evil flees.

He is the will of those who have lost their will to addiction. He is the strength of will to end addiction.

> ...may all who seek You
>   Rejoice and be glad in You.
> May those who long for your help
>   Always say, "God be glorified."
> Here I am, afflicted and poor.
>   God, come quickly.
> You are my help and deliverer.
>   Lord, do not delay!" (Psalms 70:5-6)

"There is a road meant for you to travel. Narrow and steep is the shepherd's way... There is a cross meant for you to carry...a cross meant for you alone... How many times have you doubted my word? How many times must I call your name? And as you say, "Yes," letting me love you, I will be the strength for your journey." ("Strength for the Journey," by Michael John Poirier, 1999)

Questions for discussion:

When your heart cannot forgive, can you ask God to help you? To forgive yourself? Others?

Can you turn to Him when life becomes too painful? Who or what do you turn to during difficult times? Is it successful?

If not, would you reconsider and are you ready to try another way?

Room for Thoughts

Chapter 8

* * *

The Addict

Deceived by substances promising to restore balance and to alleviate pain, the addict is as clueless as a wife who unquestioningly believes the lipstick smear on her husband's collar was left by his mother. The addict is also taken in by deceptions which ease the pain of negativity and failure—only to reaffirm the lies of unworthiness.

The "addictive personality" is a popular catch-all phrase attempting to explain life-dissatisfaction. But this simplistic term barely brushes the surface of addiction.

Who or what is an addict? Is it the individual who after another fruitless day's work denies reality in the arms of a prostitute? Or the individual who soothes their loneliness with excessive calories or drink?

Are they addicts? Are they consumed by obsessive thoughts leading to irrational or unacceptable behavior? Is their guilt sufficient to maintain addiction?

A popular song writer claims, "I'm addicted to love." Is he really addicted to love? A love-addict? Would anyone buy a song entitled, "I'm addicted to cocaine"?

The point is…we are all addicts. Our addictions or obsessive attachments involve almost every substance and thing known to mankind. But it is the power of the attachment, the dedication of energy and responsibility of behavior, that determines the potential danger of addiction—and the inability to change.

Regardless of the addiction or its influential power, its existence results from an innate need to maintain or restore balance and well-being. Consider the lengths some employ to regain satisfaction; the money spent and the lives affected by abusive practices; the guilt and the shame.

I was in a tenant's home, someone I barely knew, and there was a bowl of chocolate on the coffee table. Now I could have just asked for a piece, but I didn't. Admittedly, I am a dark chocoholic, but my action that day was irrational. When she left the room, I grabbed a handful, stuffed it in my mouth, and, still chewing, looked very guilty and embarrassed when she returned.

These learned behaviors (addictions) provide the instant, although short-term, gratification sought regardless of resulting negativity. The addictions are so powerful, their pull so immediate, that reason is bypassed and future concerns ignored because the mind is clouded by thoughts of instantaneous pleasure.

The need for balance cannot be overstated. Mind, body, and heart will do anything to retain/regain feel-good balance. This is what drives us to perform daily. This is what determines thought and behavior—all directed at filling the heart-void.

Balance is a basic human need that will not be ignored. And the mind cleverly devises substitute preoccupations in service to the heart. It is the attending physician who prolongs the patient's life without affecting a cure.

So, what is the cure?

By discovering and accepting the basic heart-need that mind and body are unable to satisfy out of ignorance (not for lack of trying), balance will be attained. Mind and body understand the satisfaction of worldly pleasures. But, since the heart is not based in the world, these pleasures are superficial entertainment.

Discover the heart's need by returning to the basics—to God's truth within our hearts.

Years ago I was guided through an imaginary journey of the mind as part of a required weekend at Duquesne University. Having no expectation, the outcome was surprising and I would like to share this journey with you.

Imagine a road stretching before you. In your mind, design the road—the surface and the surroundings. Is it straight or wandering? Imagine yourself as you begin the journey— how do you feel? What are you wearing? Can you feel the sun's warmth on your face or is it covered by clouds?

The road is unfamiliar and the destination unknown. Are you eager or hesitant? Since every journey begins with the first step, you take that step. Determine your pace as the road stretches before you.

The road is open and you can clearly see all around. Take in your surroundings. Is there a breeze? Can you hear the sound of birds and insects? Breathe deeply—can you smell the earth? Engage all your senses.

The road begins to curve slightly and you pick up your pace. Trees and foliage become denser as you enter a wooded area. Can you feel the change in temperature? As your eyes adjust to the light, are you aware of different sights? Scents? There is a large rock in the path and you pause to rest. What are you thinking? How do you feel? Are you tired? Energized? Impatient?

Continue through the forest until you reach a clearing. The road forks, forcing you to choose a new direction. Proceed, noticing any changes in the surroundings.

After traveling awhile, the road again forks, requiring another decision. And again, you must decide. Continue walking, or perhaps you would prefer to jog. Notice any changes.

The road splits one last time. You decide on a path and continue. In the distance there is a mountain. How high is the mountain? What are your thoughts?

A path leads to the top to the mountain. Begin the climb.

At the top of the mountain, a man sits. He seems familiar and you realize he is the reason for the journey. What does he look like? How is he dressed? This man has something to say—words specifically intended for you. What does he say? What were your heart-spoken words? Mine were, "Trust in God and trust in yourself."

Trust—exactly what was missing from my life. Trust in God and trust in myself—words I needed to hear. Words from my heart.

Truth comes from the heart, and when we speak from the heart, people will listen—for they recognize heart-truth. When we speak from the heart, we speak with love. God is love. So, when we speak from the heart, we speak God's truth.

* * *

The journey may have seemed long and arduous—and like many of life's journeys, filled with doubt. It was planned as our lives are planned—requiring decisions. We choose, and trusting our choices, occasionally change direction—hoping for the best outcome. Life's journey is founded on trust and hope.

* * *

"Trust in God…" Faith leads to trust and trust enables hope—the three components of love (unselfish and unconditional), to be shared with others and returned to the Originator.

God resides in the heart, and since He is love, it is love that fills the heart-void. Love is the balance we seek, the balance missing from most of our lives. This is the basis for that feel-good sensation, and no man-made substitute can equal in its power or longevity.

Love gives us worth. Love provides the means to overcome the addictive lies. Self-less love opens the heart to love self-lessly.

I have the privilege of knowing a couple (both have histories of previous marriages) who are unmistakably devoted to each other. I asked John the secret to their continuing love affair. How does he maintain the love; what does he do?

He answered, "It's simple really. My purpose, my goal in life, is to help and support my wife so she can be the best she can possibly be." (The most perfect definition of self-less love I have ever heard.)

"Trust in yourself…" All the answers ever needed are waiting within if we open the eyes of our heart. Just look to the heart to hear the words of God.

"Trust in God" enables us to trust ourselves—allowing the chance-taking necessary to develop our potential. And trusting ourselves enables us to trust others.

* * *

Commonalities among addictions: dependence on the feel-good sensation, guilt or fear associated with the behavior, and constancy of use due to the temporary nature of addictive substances. Variable factors include: visibility, social acceptance, frequency of usage, level of functioning, degree of dependency, and life-threat potential.

Addictions can be rated from "soft" (or the more acceptable forms) to "hard core." But what separates the everyday socially accepted lowercase "addict" from the socially ridiculed uppercase "Addict?" What factors are accountable for creating the "Addict?"

* * *

Early life experiences can negatively affect self-image and behavior, setting the stage for future addictive concerns. The potency of others-instilled self-image based on unrealistic expectations or positive self-affirming interactions contributes to or detracts us from achieving our God-given potential—the difference between life-satisfaction and dissatisfaction.

It is our others-instilled self-image that determines trust and self-worth, which either frees or inhibits exploration of talents and the willingness to take chances. Self-image establishes the worthiness of loving and being loved, feelings of love-unworthiness, and attitudes reflected in our treatment of self and others.

We treat others with the same respect as we treat ourselves. If we don't respect ourselves, we are incapable of respecting others. Just look at historical abuse, the everyday abuses reported as nightly commentary—the abuses in our schools and in our own homes. Such abuse is only possible through objectification—reducing people to objects by extracting humanity from mankind and denying its Divine origin.

All life is worthy of respect, from the micro-organisms existing beneath the sea to the two-legged stewards of the earth. God created life from nothing and without Him, nothing would exist.

Life without respect (without God-worth) lacks value and a valueless existence lacks meaning. And like a boat without an anchor, we wander aimlessly—occasionally slowing with life's current, but never stopping long enough to seek purpose for our seemingly meaningless existence.

Life without purpose turns to frustration and frustration to anger as we become increasingly discontent and out of balance. In search of life-resolution, it becomes commonplace to blame others for perceived inadequacies and failures since the world is an untrustworthy and hostile environment. And people, the objectified "them" of the world, become the source of our suffering.

The stage is now set for the potential making of an addict. Drowning in the lies of others, without purpose and without anchor, societal alienation begins. As a loner and sole protector of the addictive lies, care is taken to insure nonexposure of the shameful truth. Mental, emotional, and physical distance is established as the individual withdraws into an impenetrable shell. The story continues with the prioritization of personal needs, while a lifetime of unresolved emotional burdens prevents the movement of growth.

It is isolation that perpetuates the behavior—and it is the interior emptiness (heart-void) that initiates the need for the behavior (addiction).

The potential addict is caught in a downward spiral of negativity, which becomes a self-fulfilling prophesy of thought and behavior as confirmation of the original lies or others' assessment of negative self-worth. Trust is nonexistent and life is deemed hopeless. Spiraling downward in despair, life simply becomes too painful and not worth the living.

Plagued by the worthlessness of the "not enoughs," it is the shame-filled past that dictates the future, often inhibiting personal and vocational success. Outcomes are negatively predetermined and the joy of accomplishment is overridden by the fear of discovery.

Graduate degrees are never bestowed out of pity—they are earned by years of hard work and tenacity. Yet, as I waited for my name to be called, a wave of insecurity washed away the pride of accomplishment my fellow students were feeling. I felt unworthy—the token blonde in a sea of intelligence. A mistake among my classmates.

Feeling alone and unique, this individual carries a secret burden of lies, reverberating continually within his head.

The interior words, the hurtful lies, need to be silenced. Negative, debilitating thoughts need to be erased and self-hatred turned into self-love. But, without hope, this is not possible. Without hope, the promises made by addictive substances become increasingly more attractive.

The out-of-balance heart, mind, and body scream for a reprieve from years of relentless suffering. But nothing is able to kill the pain or silence the words. Nothing is able to shut out the world.

Remember that balance must be restored, and coping mechanisms developed to reestablish wellness. But since the potential addict is isolated, emotionally and physically, the usual methods of social interaction are not available and more extreme solutions (mind and emotionally altering substances) are necessary to survive one day at a time, one hour at a time, and one minute at a time. To merely survive.

But the escape-route-of-choice is not perfect as the once seemingly flawless becomes flawed, as the plan develops snags. The warning signs become increasingly difficult to ignore as discontent heightens. And then, the escape route, now seen as far from perfect, is blocked with the reemergence of pain.

The world loudly returns as the peace of nothingness fades into memory. Relief for the addict was but a fading dream. A haven for the sick at heart. A fleeting and imperfect restoration of balance.

Addictive substances are mere cover-ups for the illness of the heart, providing a false sensation of well-being. Due to the nature of the prescription, it must be administered often for pain reduction—creating an endless cycle of self-medication.

For addicts, the small blue window of hope is clouded with despair. And without concern for tomorrow, the addict functions solely in the present, seeking quick and effective release from a past so painful that it controls the present and the future.

Stuck in the past, addicts function on a level of emotional immaturity, suggesting that at some point in their developmental history, time simply stood still.

"It is the nature of one who has self-centered desires to be ever discontented and dissatisfied." This quote by St. Teresa of Avila rephrases the words of St. John of the Cross during the 16th century. Restated in 21st century terms: contentment and satisfaction are improbable when 24/7 is dedicated to self-absorption—the "I" mentality.

The addict resides in the addiction like a turtle resides within the confines of its shell—alone and frightened like an abandoned child whose fate is sealed by false and demanding gods.

Caught within the cycle and blinded to options, it seems easier to maintain addictive behavior than to reach out for help. So, still clinging to the security blanket of addiction, that hand is never extended. And as long as the blanket is within reach, it never will be.

When you subscribe to the "not-enoughs," and believe the cascade of imperfections bestowed by others, failure is inevitable. Failure is taught. It is a learned behavior and not the normal human conclusion. Failure is limiting for it negates trying and thus negates succeeding. Positive thinking leads to positive outcome, and negative thought leads to failure. If failure is the expectation, failure will happen through failure-generated behavior.

Addiction's will is absolute. Through lies it empowers a false sense of security and control. But the addict is never in control and the feel-good sensations only mask the growing dependency. A dependency powerful enough to usurp pride and free-will through thought and behavioral control—mimicking the desired state of well-being while accepting nothing in exchange. Nothing, that is, except the addict's life.

Change is difficult for many individuals because change elicits the scary element of unpredictability. Knowing when and what to expect is comfortable for it takes the guess work as well as the surprise out of life. Behaviors are learned, automatically dictating and transferring responses between similar situations. And once learned, the response is elicited without the stress of conscious decision making.

Similar life events evoke similar reactions, explaining the occasional irresistible charm of that pint of Baskin-Robbins ice cream nestled toward the back of the freezer between the frozen broccoli spears and the chicken. This emotional food-connection may have originated when Mom soothed the pain of a skinned knee with a double scoop of mint chocolate chip. And you felt better. You felt loved.

Food satisfies both physical and emotional needs. Consider the phrase "comfort food"—we associate certain foods with good times and good memories. Linking food with feeling good, we have learned to reach for the satisfaction of food during periods of discontent. We have learned that pasta soothes a broken heart and pizza cures Friday night loneliness. A sore throat warrants a lollipop and chicken soup cures whatever else is ailing.

We eat in happiness, in sadness, and in sickness. We eat socially and we eat alone in the privacy of our homes. We can over-eat or under-eat. We can eat healthy or junk food. Carnivore or vegetarian, it is our choice, for food not only fills an empty stomach, but an empty heart as well.

There is a line of demarcation between using and abusing substances. And food, like all self-medicating substances, can become addictive. For the over-eater, food becomes the drug of choice.

There are many drugs of choice, all intended to make us feel better. Substances that fill the emptiness and the interior hollow echoing of past, present, and future failure. Substances that attempt to restore balance to the mind, body, and heart.

The addict has lost all freedom, except one—the mental cunning of procurement; the ability to pretend, to lie and steal in order to perpetuate the habit.

* * *

It is said that the addict needs to hit rock bottom before recovery or self-rediscovery is possible, and lose everything of societal value—relationships, pride, finances, home, family, and security.

This implies the loss of everything with the exception of life—the addict's only remaining possession, and that, unfortunately, is devoid of meaning.

It is said that when you hit rock bottom the only way is up—although the addict has lost direction and hasn't a clue which way is up.

I hit my rock bottom at a detox facility in Western Pennsylvania. Confined within its walls, I finally, after many years of denial, faced the reality of my addiction. The truth could no longer be denied: I needed to change.

For me, the shocking reality was the loss of freedom. I felt like a caged animal and signed my release after only three days of confinement.

Eventually, addiction becomes a choice between life and death—the mindless, permanent solution to all concerns. An appealing solution compared to the present level of pain and the likelihood of continuing pain without drastic life change. And without change, recovery is as ill-fated as attempting to stem a leak in Hoover Dam with bubble gum. It just won't work.

Change begins by acknowledging certain truths: (1) as members of the human race, we are not perfect; (2) we make mistakes; (3) our control over life is limited—life happens with or without our consent; (4) we cannot control others—the best we can do is accept responsibility for our own behavior; and (5) WE NEED GOD.

"I will sprinkle clean water upon you to cleanse you from your impurities and from all your idols will I cleanse you. I will give you a new heart and place a new spirit within you" (Ezekiel 36:25-26).

Humanity is weak, but it is in weakness that strength is found—if we reach out, extending our hands in grateful anticipation of a strength greater than our own.

A God-intervention is needed. Sufferers of addiction need only to raise their eyes and hands to grasp the hand of the Divine—and softly call His name. He will hear. And in hearing, He will answer.

And He did. Thank God.

In weakness, He is strength. In despair, He is hope. In loneliness, He is unconditional love.

Questions for discussion:

What are your attachments? Are they considered excessive by others? By yourself? Is guilt a factor?

Do these attachments detrimentally affect your well-being? Do they overpower your desire to change?

Do you respect yourself and others?

How do you view your future?

Do you blame others for your failures? Who taught you to fail?

Do you feel alienated from society—alone and unique? Explain.

Define addiction. Are you an addict?

What is your addiction? Does it positively or negatively influence in your life? List the pros and cons of addiction.

Room for Thoughts

Chapter 9

* * *

Life Was Never Meant to Be a Cakewalk

"Peace I leave with you; my peace I give to you. Not as the world gives do I give it to you. Do not let your hearts be troubled or afraid" (John 14:27).

An examination of these words reveals God's intention—life was never meant to be a cakewalk and the bottom line is...life's tough and everyone gets rained on.

God does not distinguish between individuals to receive the worst or the best in life, but distributes both equally. We are challenged with roadblocks and blessed with abundance in order to strengthen our love and dependency upon the Divine.

Peace is tentative at best as nations and people clash over infringements of perceived rights and honored traditions. But, even more unnerving, are the crimes committed closer to home.

Because of faulty communication and erroneous assumptions, intolerable behavior exists within families and between spouses. Is there no peace?

God is peace. It is in and through Him that we find lasting peace, for it exists nowhere else. His is the peace that dwells within our hearts and rules our thoughts and behavior—if we allow ourselves to turn inward and accept that peace.

Unlike worldly peace, God's peace is not fleeting. There are no ups and downs, for God's peace is as constant as His love.

If judged on our sins alone and the sins of humanity, we would be found sorely undeserving of God's gracious caring. But he does care because we are His creations.

If life were Utopia, God's presence would be unnecessary. But that was never the intention—for God, like all of us, desires to be needed. He wants to be loved and as a lover, He showers His beloved with precious gifts. He wants to be present in our lives.

Hope is essential. Hope is motivational. We hope for goodness. We hope for a better day. We hope in God's love and promises. Hope is faith in the "something more."

There has to be more, more to the existence of life as we know it—a purpose for the burden of the crosses we carry. Something more than our desire for control and possessions. Something more than the everyday superficiality of living.

* * *

Addiction is not a life calling. It is not a goal one actively ascribes toward. It is not the culmination of a lifelong search to achieve self-potential and become the best we can be.

But, addiction is a choice. The first drink or the first fix is a choice (perhaps taken experimentally or because of peer pressure), but a choice made without thought of emotional dependency—the lure of feeling good without regard for the beguiling powers of addiction.

The first drink or the first fix is always a choice. But, to the addict, the second is not. The immediate surge of pleasure is emotionally intoxicating, although the intensity lasts only a few seconds. After that, addiction takes over and the extremely pleasurable becomes necessity. It is important to distinguish addiction from active addiction—the distinction is the ability to say "no" and simply walk away. In active addiction, this choice does not exist.

No one strives for the label of "addict" or to be caught in its downward spiral of self-destruction. Yet it happens because addictive substances provide the balance and the happiness missing in life.

We become addicted to the emotions and the feeling of wellness elicited by addictive substances. We become addicted to feelings lacking in our lives, feelings that complete and make us whole.

An emotional bond is formed that becomes harder and harder to resist until resistance becomes futile—"puppetizing" the will with more lies until the addictive substance becomes mother, father, sister, and brother—satisfying all needs and desires. It is the one friend who never disappoints—yet the friend creating the greatest roadblock to living.

If road blocks are opportunities for change in disguise, why isn't addiction merely another obstacle or roadblocks to overcome? Since man has free will of action and thought, why can't free-will decision end addiction?

Addiction usurps free will, burying it beneath promises of feel-good wellness—the balance lacking in most lives. Presenting itself as the ultimate solution to perceived inadequacies (the accepted lies), it fulfills the hope in life's "something more," but also it inevitably reduces hope to the despair of nothingness.

Possibilities die without hope as the addict is caught in an endless cycle of self-abuse, failure, and disappointment. Addiction becomes a self-perpetuating obstacle too exhaustive to surmount, as surrender becomes the greater reality.

Addiction leaves an emotional scar so intense that it colors everything with a sense of powerlessness. We feel that life has no goodness to offer and that we have lost our place in the world. And this is what robs us of energy and our connection with others.

We are not failures because we have failed. We disappoint, but we are not disappointments. We hurt, but we are not hurtful. We simply are members of an imperfect humanity.

Yet, we are God's Beloved despite our behavior, despite our belief otherwise.

God never gives up on us, never abandons us—for abandonment is a human trait.

Addiction is life without hope—the main ingredient that fuels the fire of addiction.

Questions for discussion:

What are your "something mores" in life?

What is missing from your life?

Does addiction fill what is missing? What are the voids in your life?

Do you recognize the addiction cycle in your life? Self abuse? Failure? Despair? Other things?

Do you feel powerless?

Hopeless?

Are you really?

Room for Thoughts

Chapter 10

* * *

Balancing Mind, Body, and Heart

All three components—mind, body, and heart—must be maintained in a state of balance. This is done either naturally or is substance-induced. They must be in unison. If one is off, the remaining two are affected. Balance is necessary for well-being and for mental and physical health.

Due to the mind's penchant (ego) for pride-based control, it has the capability of overriding heart and body needs with constant reminders of the addictive lies. It is the strongest (most willful) of the three components and derives its power from imbalance.

Since the heart is the main focus, the life of our lives, it is the component the mind attempts to placate. Although mostly ignorant of heart-needs, the mind presumes to know what is pleasing—while in reality, it often substitutes its own prideful needs for the desires of this soft-spoken entity.

There is no substitute for God-centered love—the self-less giving and receiving of love without motive or expectation. It is what the heart desires and cannot be replaced by worldly offerings. No amount of treasure and no earthly passion can provide such lasting contentment.

Yet the mind employs its tainted reality to manipulate the heart's need for love through the justification of its own controlling needs. And by recalling past situations that spawned the addictive lies, it justifies its behavior.

Growth and change take place in the light of truth—truth hidden within the heart and denied by the mind. So the individual, functioning in the dark, is unable to change and is forced to relive and repeat past mistakes, forced to believe the lie of unworthiness as God's Beloved.

No matter what I accomplished, I always felt inadequate, as if the accomplishment was achieved out of default or just plain luck. I felt that if people knew the real me, the grotesque me buried within, I would be shunned. This sense of unworthiness, permeating all arenas of life, was especially dominant on the personal front as failed relationships became the norm.

The Balanced Mind

We all have a purpose that incorporates uniqueness of given talents performed as only we uniquely can. It is this individuality that distinguishes and differentiates us from others, calling us to be individuals with purpose.

Some purposes are highly visible, affecting many lives. Others, hidden from daily scrutiny, are equally challenging and satisfying. Whatever the position, regardless of earning power or visibility, all provide the satisfaction associated with doing what we were intended to do—our purpose or life's call.

Considering individual strengths and weaknesses, this calling is the materialization of the visible truth of who we are, without lies, pretenses, or fear of discovery. It is honesty in action as we fulfill the roles we were intended to play in service to others.

* * *

The balanced mind is noncontrolling—it is accepting. It derives its strength through honest self-assessment and not through the degradation of others. It is not foot-stomping willful, but capable of letting others take the forefront. It is capable of and not diminished by seeking assistance. It also admits dependency on One greater than itself.

The balanced mind harbors no past resentments, it is open to new ideas and possibilities, and it believes in its own goodness and the goodness of others. It respects the sanctity of all life and views the world as a friendly place. It is not fear-ridden and does not acknowledge its innate human weakness, but rather, it trusts and hopes in the Divine.

The balanced mind is able to take chances. It is able to take that leap of faith, that voyage into the unknown—full of hope for a positive outcome. Fearlessly trusting in God's goodness, it believes in its ability (combined with God's strength) to accomplish all that is required.

Cognizant of the truth, the balanced mind is free of guilt and able to accept responsibility for failure without blaming others. Through honest self-assessment, it is capable of change, for it is not cemented in the past and it is able to determine what works and what does not. It is also capable of changing dysfunctional or hurtful thoughts and behaviors into positive thoughts and actions dedicated to self-growth.

Realistic in its expectations, the balanced mind looks within its abilities to find its unique life's call. By accepting growth opportunities, it develops to become the best it can be in service to others, growing more Christ-like in perfection each day.

It cannot be persuaded toward evil or hurtful actions, for it knows its self-worth and joyfully accepts its status as God's Beloved. It also strives to be deserving of this by freely and completely giving of itself without expectation of anything in return.

The balanced mind anticipates new beginnings, viewing each day as an opportunity to do God's will. With a spirit of adventure, it prepares for the unknown, and God's daily surprises for each day are truly an adventure if we allow them to unfold without pre-formed and joy-robbing judgment.

It's all about perception. If we think positive thoughts, like magnets, we will attract positivity. The opposite is also true—when we expect bad things to happen, they will.

The balanced mind has respect for life and passion for living. Since God created all that exists, it recognizes and respects the work of the Almighty from conception to death. Passion is the thrill derived from knowing we are exactly in the right place at exactly the right time, and using our unique talents to do exactly what we were intended to do.

When the mind accepts the heart's love-truth and when this love-truth is made visible, we are at our unique best. This is when the boundaries between mind and heart are removed and we perform as God's Beloved.

The Unbalanced Mind

Life-dissatisfaction, that nagging feeling of unrest and the constant search for "something more," plagues the unbalanced mind. It is a fruitless search destined to endless dissatisfaction because the "something more" cannot be found in advanced technology, new wave spiritualism, infidelity, or in the acquisition of the always bigger and better. The "something more" in life is beyond man's creation—for it already exists.

We seek to please ourselves with pretty and expensive toys—and like children, we are easily distracted by the bright, the shiny, and the new. That which is pleasing catches our eyes, while the obvious is often overlooked.

Self-centered pleasures and goals, once achieved, tarnish quickly. Having little lasting power, the "something mores" cause the seeker to seek still more—always more, for the satisfaction never lives up to expectation.

With anticipation, we open a box containing five hundred pieces to a jigsaw puzzle and begin sorting colors and patterns. As the puzzle takes shape, we work faster as the pieces fall into place. Anticipation grows as the few remaining pieces easily connect. The 499th piece is placed. One hole remains. And no matter how frantically we search, the hole remains for the 500th piece of the puzzle is missing from the box.

The anticipated satisfaction is lost. We feel crushed with the realization that the final puzzle piece is missing—the final piece that would have given meaning to the hours spent working on the puzzle. We are disappointed because one piece is missing—the "something more."

There was always a gnawing uneasiness. I knew something was missing in my life but could not identify the missing piece. I looked, trying to find that piece in helping others— thinking that perhaps better understanding would lead to understanding myself. I admired the peace and graciousness in certain individuals, yearning to find the source.

For the unbalanced mind, there is always one piece of the puzzle missing. Always one piece—the anticipated piece that deprives the satisfaction of completing the whole picture.

Pleasure-based happiness provides the quick fix that society is drawn toward. But these substance-less pleasures (those attractive to the mind because they feed the ego) are merely attempts to create balance and well-being. They are self- (mind) and not heart-originated.

The unbalanced mind blames others for its unhappiness and dissatisfaction. The puzzle manufacturer sells inferior products and doesn't deserve to be in business; the store should deal with more reputable manufacturers; someone during inspection should have noticed that a piece was missing. Everyone is blamed, except for the unbalanced mind, who simply neglected to look under the sofa for the missing piece.

Imbalance is empowerment for the unbalanced mind. And satisfaction lies in life's orchestration—the attempted control of situations and others. Although control is illusion, the unbalanced mind will incorporate such tactics as persuasion, power, bribery—whatever it takes to maintain its sense of control and its sense of well-being. And although it thrives on power, satisfaction always remains beyond reach.

A void exists, and although vaguely aware of the void, the unbalanced mind will still continue its controlling behavior by attempting to fill the void. It will also continue as acquisitions are stuffed into the void in order to ease the emptiness while ignoring the origin of the dissatisfaction—the starvation of the heart.

The Balanced Body

As a God-given vessel that houses the soul, the body deserves respect. It is a creation of brilliance whose functionality is incomparable to anything mankind has or ever will devise.

Our internal and external structures, far more complex than the loftiest of human imaginings, are as unique as snowflakes. No two individuals are identical in appearance or ability.

Considering the billions of people inhabiting the earth, this concept of uniqueness is mind-boggling. Yet, as unique as we are, we all possess one basic commonality—we are all the beloved children of God.

We are all equally loved and valued—valued by God as His one-of-a-kind creations. In the eyes of God we all possess great worth; yet in the eyes of man, we are often devalued. If we believed the truth within our hearts, lives would change. If we believed our God-worthiness, our life and the lives of others would reflect the reverence befitting our origin.

Respecting life means respect-filled living derived from God, who is love. We are called to love one another as we are loved. And since love breeds respect, we are called to treat ourselves and others with the respect owed a God-creation.

Respect implies caring for the personal welfare of self and others. It rejects self-abuse and negative self-judgment. Respect disallows the abuse and devaluation of others.

Life begins and ends in God. He made us who we are. We determine who we become.

* * *

Healthy maintenance allows the balanced body to function efficiently at will. And considering the complexity of systems involved, surprisingly little is required.

If a body receives adequate love, it is able to give and receive love. If it receives periodic maintenance to ensure health, it is able to give and receive comfort and pleasure.

A balanced body requires no added substances to feel good, for the accompanying sense of health and well-being provide a natural high. This feel-good sensation, resulting from self-love and respect, provides the energizing motivation to exercise and eat properly.

The Unbalanced Body
Currently in the U.S. food abuse is a major population concern. Food-related addictions are prevalent within all age groups of the population, regardless of social, racial, or economic status. It is estimated that 8 million Americans have an eating disorder—this is more prevalent in the female population: 7 million compared to 1 million men.

One in 200 American women (and 95% of these are between the ages of 12 and 25) suffer from anorexia. Two to three in every 100 are bulimic.

Fifty-eight million Americans are overweight. Forty million are obese. And three million have been categorized as morbidly obese.

The long and short-term effects of food abuse are seen daily in doctors' offices and behind closed doors. Ranging from joint replacements and diabetes to emotional and physical self-abuse, over-eating and under-eating are attempts to regain balance. They are physical manifestations of unresolved emotional issues—a substitution or denial of food for love and self-respect.

The USDA has established nutritional guidelines to assist individuals in establishing and maintaining a healthy and well-balanced diet. These guidelines are taught in schools. Posters array the walls of most doctors' offices and health clinics, yet are largely ignored because the problems lie not in the food, for food, like all addictions, is merely a catalyst to provide what is missing—life-balance.

It is understood that working parents and commitments diminish kitchen time for today's family, unlike past eras when homemaking was not a career option and family sit-down dinners were a daily occurrence. And meals were prepared, if not with love, with time-consuming regularity. Today, this tradition rarely exists and many family members are left to fend for themselves.

It is difficult to always include the right foods into our diet. At times it is easier to stop at that fast food restaurant specializing in empty calories loaded with salt, sugars, and fats—the foods responsible for the unprecedented obesity rate in this country.

What is consumed is reflected in the body's sense of well-being. The old saying is true—you are what you eat. Fat produces fat. Sugar produces fast energy which ultimately leads to a crash if not supplemented by more stable carbs. And high levels of sodium can lead to disease. Poor nutrition takes a physical toll on the body, on its efficient functioning, on its feel-goodness.

Most Americans are hooked on fast food. Note the number of children in McDonalds or Burger King restaurants consuming hamburger, fries, and soda. Guaranteed: they will be sitting at the same tables as unhealthy and overweight adults.

We have become a sedentary generation. It was reported that children spend as much as eight hours daily at computer-related activities. No wonder childhood obesity, once unknown in the U.S., has become disturbingly prevalent. Obese children become obese adults who equate the fullness of food with the feel-goodness of love.

Daily physical exercise, in addition to good nutrition, is an essential component of a balanced body. Exercise makes us feel good by increasing the levels of mood-elevating neurochemicals such as endorphins, so we feel better mentally and physically.

During the day we sit at our desks. And at night before the TV munching on pizza and chips. We know the right choices for a healthy, balanced body, yet often make the wrong choices, those providing the same short-lived satisfaction of addiction.

Like all addictions, food abuse is initially voluntary. No one is forced to overeat, under-eat, over-exercise, or avoid exercise like the plague. It is the satisfaction, the need for balance, that is addicting. The overall sense of pleasure that creates the repetitive behavior. The feel-goodness most lives crave and are lacking. Substitutes for love and self-worth in the form of cream-filled éclairs and double meat and cheese burgers. Or exhaustive daily workouts to prove physical desirability.

We abuse our bodies by what is consumed or withheld. We neglect our bodies when simple maintenance is all that is required. We are a society of excess and excess is addicting.

The night was warm as I leaned out of my bedroom window, lighting my first cigarette. I inhaled tentatively and coughed profusely. Although it tasted as badly as it smelled, I persevered, for it was the "cool" (social acceptance) grown-up thing to do. My lungs hurt, my throat burned, and my stomach churned, but I felt "cool," until seconds later, leaning farther out the window, I vomited. That was not "cool," but persistence pays and the next evening when I tried again I maintained my "cool."

* * *

Whatever the addiction—food, drugs, alcohol, sex, cosmetic surgery, nicotine, etc.—all exist as extreme behavioral attempts (self-medication) at restoration of normalcy or balance. Nothing more than fleeting pleasures, these ill-fated behaviors attempt to fill emotional voids in ignorance of what is truly missing from our lives.

The pace of life has increased as we cram increasingly more activities into our waking hours. We have no patience for traffic delays. We have no time to wait in line without complaints escalating into abusive words and behavior.

We are instant gratification junkies—drive-thru services, microwaveable foods, etc. Addiction provides instant gratification.

The unbalanced body is in a chronic state of malaise. Plagued by such physical symptoms as lack of energy, aches, fatigue, and tension, a generalized sense of unwellness prevails. Digestive upset resulting in constipation, bloating, and excessive production of gas may acerbate the condition.

The symptoms are real, not imaginings of the mind, and can be debilitating to the extent of affecting life-quality. Consider the over-the-counter and prescription drugs available to calm nerves and relieve physical discomfort.

The Balanced Heart

Joy-filled, the balanced heart experiences life through the eyes of love. As a seeker, it uncovers the silver lining in situations and goodness in people. It finds love in the utterance of a single word or the touch of a hand. And at times, the joy is so intense, the heart is near bursting.

How could it be otherwise, if God resides within the heart? It is truly the greatest joy to hear His voice and feel His presence. Or to smile at the gentleness of His touch and delight in the daily surprises He sends as reassurance of His continuing love-commitment.

The balanced heart becomes more God-centered as the "I" fades from thought, word, and behavior and we no longer reign supreme in our self-centered worlds. Reducing the "I" mentality frees us from the stress of control, the pressure to orchestrate ourselves and others in the dance of life—which we ultimately discover is beyond our talents anyway.

Once the mind acknowledges its limitations and releases its illusionary control, the heart awakens to the joy-filled possibilities of living. It is freed to trust and love, to acknowledge its God-base, and to give of itself in service to others,

Love resides where the Lord resides. He is love. His love is unconditional and everlasting, unwavering regardless of our wavering inconsistencies.

The balanced heart abandons itself to the Divine and in total trust accepts a will greater than its own. It is not forced acceptance, nor the result of deep despair, but an overt acceptance of love. And when the heart opens to love, joy ultimately follows.

Human will, based in pride, opposes relinquishing control. It opposes the concept of subservience. But, that's what is required of us—to become servants. This is a word of historically negative connotation, a word offensive to a nation who continues to fight for independence.

But, if we substitute the phrase "to serve," the request becomes more palatable. By substituting a verb for a noun, the personification of servant is removed, showcasing the action to serve a more socially acceptable pursuit.

We are called to serve one another in love by offering ourselves and our talents without expectation. Providing service creates a "high" beyond equal—a "high" without the shame or guilt of substance abuse.

The addict serves no one but the addiction.

"Pride goes before disaster and a haughty spirit before a fall (Proverbs 16:18)," a familiar biblical quote, addresses the falsehood of man's pride. Pride is mind-willfulness exhibited through physical acts of control. It is a cover-up for human weakness, denying dependency upon a greater Force. Pride separates us from God, for it blocks His love.

The balanced heart trusts in God's goodness. And like a trusting child, fears no harm, knowing the Almighty will provide guidance, comfort, and strength in times of duress.

The balanced heart is hope-filled. Regardless of what happens in life, no matter what obstacles are presented, the balanced heart knows all will be well.

As one of God's Beloved, it acknowledges its right and worthiness to be loved. Open to love, the balanced heart is self- and others-accepting. It shares itself freely without fear of judgment and is willing to take chances because it is hope-filled.

It sees beauty in a world that so often overlooks beauty. In a world too busy to notice perfection in a flower or the contentment in a woman's eyes. It swells with joy at a sunset and swoons at the laughter of a child. And sees the reflection of God in others.

The balanced heart is love-filled and requires no external stimuli nor false "highs" to feel complete, for it is already complete. God completes us with His love and when the heart opens His presence is known.

The Unbalanced Heart

Emptiness is the main characteristic of the unbalanced heart. Even in the best of circumstances, it finds little pleasure in life's pursuit of the pleasures that ultimately fall short of the mark.

It knows the truth. It knows what is lacking, but is unable to communicate because the mind's voice brays too loudly. Sorrowed by debilitating loss, the unbalanced heart slowly dies, closing itself to the love needed for survival.

Instinctively, the heart knows what is missing and is not impressed by the mind's controlling bravado as defense against the truth, as defense against its own inability to control. And the weak, longing sighs of the heart remain unheard amid the thunder of superficiality.

The most willful and the loudest of the three components, the mind decides, as self-proclaimed caretaker of the heart and body, what is best. While presuming to know the heart's needs, it actually attempts to please, but hasn't a clue, for the mind is worldly based. It attempts to please by restoring balance with materialistic pleasures.

This love-less, malnourished heart meekly accepts the lies of the mind, for it hasn't the strength to articulate the truth. And a void is created, stifling the heart's Light.

The heart cannot breathe. It can barely beat for the pain of abandonment.

The heart's vision is clouded by despair. Unable to see clearly, its Light dimmed and all but extinguished. It is empty without love, without the hope of love.

The unbalanced heart beats with the pain of despair.

Questions for discussion:

Are you content? What provides your contentment?

Can you identify repetitive behaviors that lead to unhappiness?

When engaging your unique talents, how do you feel? Might these talents indicate a potential life-purpose? Explain.

What are your addictive lies?

Can you change your thinking and behavior? Can you accept responsibility for the truth?

What is your truth?

Can you acknowledge your worth and accept your role as one of God's Beloved?

Room for Thoughts

Chapter 11

* * *

Where Did It All Start?
Let's Go Back to the Beginning
and With God's Help and
Understanding, Revisit the Past

Sitting in a beauty salon, I overheard a conversation between the shop owner and an older woman who went unnoticed. The shop owner apologized for the oversight, commenting that the woman was "just so quiet. I didn't even know you were there."
"Yes," she replied. "I'm a good girl."

Now where did that come from? Where did she learn that being quiet means being good? How did she come to equate the two behaviors?

A child comes home in tears with a skinned knee. He receives no sympathy and is told to behave like a man and suck it up. The next time he is hurt, he internalizes the pain and emotion. Years later, his emotionless life is shattered by divorce.

The report card shows all A's with one exception—a B- in math. Instead of the appropriate pride-filled response, attention is focused on the lower math grade. Still striving for perfection, the now grown child is unable to find stability and satisfaction in private and professional life for he/she will never attain the unattainable—the perfect report card boasting all A's.

His parents are fighting and he feels responsible. Perhaps if he behaved or listened better. Perhaps if he was never born, there would be no fighting. He feels guilt. He feels worthless— negative feelings he carries into adulthood, affecting the quality of life.

We learn from parents and caregivers, accurately or inaccurately, who and what we are by verbal and behavioral messages transmitted either by loving affirmation or by words tinged with disgust and actions severe with impatience. These messages are internalized and impact the child's worth-identity.

It is a child's nature to please. We learn what to do and how to act by the positive and negative reactions of others. We learn who we are by how we are treated. We learn our worthiness or worthlessness through the care received.

Parents and caregivers are the first teachers who determine the pattern for our lives. If we are shown to be disgusting, inadequate little creatures, this self-image will prevail. If we are shown love, we learn to love and trust in our goodness and the goodness around us.

Positive and negative messages provide the basis for development. And depending on the messages, a child will either grow into a capable, functioning member of society or a society-draining emotional handicap.

Our journey begins prior to birth and we are the sum total of all experiences gathered along the way. Some experiences are good and affect us positively. Others leave us wounded and scarred. But all remain to influence our thoughts and behaviors.

If we are shown love, we learn to love ourselves and others. If our care is consistent and affirming, we learn to trust self and others in a world perceived as nonthreatening. Trust develops into hope as each day presents opportunities for growth-filled change, challenging our talents. And each day becomes an adventure filled with God's loving surprises.

Love, trust, and hope are the three components essential for life-satisfaction. Yet, these three components elude many of us.

Raised with negativity, our vision becomes negative. Our sense of self becomes negative. Words and actions hurt. Words and actions affixed as permanent, lifelong labels—nonremovable regardless of the amount of scrubbing and hot water. And the labels read: *Rejected: This product is of inferior quality and does not meet parental standards and expectations.*

Farfetched? Not really. If we believe the contents of our package are spoiled, we are certain everyone knows and can identify us by the foul smell. And there is just no hiding from the putrid contents of ourselves.

And as a worthless product, there is no reason to change. How sad. Yet, that's how many of us feel. And feelings translate to action—the action of no action.

As products of inferior quality, we self-reject, dismissing potential for change. We are who we were told we are and there is no changing that, so we simply accept our fate. We deserved to fail, for we are failures, and anything suggesting otherwise is incorrect, so wrong that our minds often create self-destructive scenarios. And when something bad happens, we readily accept blame; after all, it is our fault as inferior products.

As spoiled merchandise, it is easier to accept blame instead of taking a critical look at the circumstances to determine the truth. Self-doubt and self-rejection distort our vision of reality. We fail because we expect to fail—that is what we do—and we do it so well.

Thus, the self-fulfilling prophesy—I fail because I am no good; I am no good, therefore I fail.

Now, having established where the negativity and mistruths originate, the question arises: "What do we do about it?"

Questions for discussion:

Did you feel loved as a child? Rejected? Explain.

Do you consider yourself a failure? Do you expect to fail?

Can you accept blame when things go wrong?

As a product, rate yourself. Would consumers purchase you? Why? Why not?

Room for Thoughts

Part Two

Chapter 12

* * *

So, What Do We Do?

Revisiting the Past to Change the Future

To learn the truth, we must go back to the beginning, when and where the lies originated. But we can't go alone. We must go back armed with the knowledge of God's unconditional love. With open hearts and our hand in His, we go not to confront, but to acknowledge the source, the originators of the lies. We go back with love and understanding, expressing our gratitude for the opportunity to reclaim our rightful lives.

And what is rightfully ours? Love and respect by self and others—our established birthright as children of God. Love and respect—two things inherent in life, yet so easily dismissed by life.

When we are loved, we learn to love. When we are respected, we learn to respect the sanctity of life.

Without love and respect, life loses value and humans are objectified. And as objects, easily replaceable. We become things without identity, without souls. And within this mind-set, euthanasia, abortion, and killing all becomes acceptable.

We don't respect others, for the addictive lies have taught us not to respect ourselves.

As victims of the lie-tellers, we feel betrayed by those who are supposed to love us. And we feel angry and disappointed.

Investigation reveals that we are not the sole victims in this scenario, but victims of those previously victimized—our parents and caregivers. Victimization is generational and like us, they have suffered. And they will continue to suffer until they, like us, seek to regain their birthright.

Perhaps perfection exists in another universe, certainly not in ours, for perfection is beyond human acquisition. We reach, perhaps even sense it within our grasp, yet it eludes us as we delude ourselves into believing our capacity for perfection.

Yet, the goal is always within sight to inspire. No one is perfect. I am not perfect. You are not perfect. Our parents and caregivers are/were not perfect.

We all have limitations. We all have faults and weaknesses. If we didn't, we would be in the god-category. And if we were gods, there would be no need for the Divine.

We are not gods and were never intended to be. We are humans with all the frailties of humankind, equally capable of loving and hating. We unintentionally and sometimes, intentionally, hurt others. We hurt ourselves. Our perception of reality is jaded and the perception of our weaknesses is often more debilitating than the actual limitation itself.

Perception is personal, the glasses through which life is viewed; rose-colored or smudged with years of grime; unwashed glasses limiting reality and achievement.

Perception is subjective for we become who we think we are based on the perception of others. Perception judgmentally flawed and biased in its limitation. And it is up to us to decide our strengths and weaknesses instead of accepting lies told by the grimy glass wearers. It is up to us to wash our own glasses for a better look at our reality.

Excess Baggage—the Addictive Lies

Most of us play to our audience with masks affixed to disguise our true identity, the feared inner-self. And like makeup, the masks are more or less artfully applied depending upon our sense of security. They are the visible fulfillment of the addictive lies capable of disguising our inadequacy.

Those who suffer from addiction wear no masks, making no pretenses to be anything but addicts. There is nothing to hide, no illusions to maintain, for they no longer seek society's approval. They have disconnected—aliens in a world that formed them.

"Excess baggage" is a commonly used term. We understand its meaning and acknowledge its life-burden. It slows us down, thwarting our efforts and making life harder than necessary. It serves no positive purpose, yet most of us carry excess baggage or addictive lies (the perceptions of others that we believe, and in believing propagate) with or without knowing.

Although originally packed for us, most individuals possess the ability to sort through the excessive baggage and repack depending upon need and occasion. We can pull out or replace certain items at will. In other words, we have the key to open and refasten the lock. We have the ability to change what is in the bag.

The addict lacks control over the contents of his baggage, the items packed since childhood. He cannot rummage through and select those best serving his purpose and rid those hindering progress. He lacks the ability to dispute others—reality carried within the bag.

Addiction captures the addict's will and holds it ransom for the promise of another fix. The addict is like a puppet and the addiction the puppeteer that manipulates the strings.

Hope is the byproduct of trust. And since trust doesn't exist for the addict, hope does not exist. But, hope is essential for overcoming addiction—the hope of something better. And it is only when trusting in Another—whose strength is without equal—that hope becomes reality.

Without hope, tomorrow doesn't exist for the addict, only today and only the moment. Momentary survival with one objective—free from pain. Freedom: that precious numbness that surrounds like a protective shield.

Societal normalcy, defined within the realm of daily activities, provides little interest to the addict whose world revolves in a lazy, pain-free blur. In this haze-filled existence, dancing to its own tune, little else has meaning.

* * *

Change involves stepping outside one's comfort zone. But, as creatures of habit, it is often more desirable to maintain predictability, despite the negativity of a situation, than to change.

Life-predictability reduces the element of the unknown that we as controllers seek to avoid. There is tremendous comfort in knowing what to expect.

Situational discomfort usually signals the need for change; the greater the discomfort, the greater the need for change. By ignoring signals, we deny growth opportunities that allow the exploration of untried potential. Denial inhibits the development of God-given talents and blinds us to future possibilities. Change is the acknowledged rational decision made when the situational discomfort outweighs the degree of comfort in a given situation.

Emotional discomfort, although also signaling the need for change, appears more resistant to change. Unhealthy long-term relationships, for example, are maintained regardless of chronic pain. Repetitive behaviors, although detrimental to individual wellness, are maintained, and like Linus in Charlie Brown, we cling to these security blankets of ineffectiveness.

Once the decision is made, most individuals are capable of change. But those with addictions are not—for the addict must first "hit rock bottom," thus forcing the decision.

It is only when the pain of remaining the same becomes greater than the fear of change that change will occur.

* * *

The suitcase remains locked for the key has been lost. The object now is to find the key and unlock the suitcase—a difficult task, but with God's strength, possible. Once we do all that is humanly possible, trusting in the goodness of God, we leave the rest to Him.

* * *

The addict's journey becomes more perilous due to false bottoming—when it doesn't seem possible to sink any farther, the elevator descends to yet a lower floor of despair and hopelessness. And it will continue to descend until that final bump as it settles on the basement floor. At "rock bottom," the elevator, like the addict, can sink no lower.

This is the final destination for the addict. Stripped bare of relationships, family, pride, and dignity, only one possession remains—life. And a life or death choice must be made. Change must occur along with a commitment to live—for the only other choice is death.

Commitment to change comes from the desperation of choosing life over death.

* * *

Daily journaling is recommended as an ongoing documentation of insights into the past, present, and future. Write a commitment prayer and repeat it often.

* * *

By now it is assumed that you are committed to ending the pain of addiction and to understand the relationship between mind, body, and heart. You understand the mind's well-intended but faulty assessment of the heart's unarticulated need and the importance of satisfying that need. Since the heart is the center of our being, its wellness is of prime concern. Balance is the goal—the restoration of naturally induced, abuse-free wellness. Balance provides the strength and impetus for living addiction-free as one of God's beloved.

Hope and trust in God provides the courage for change. He is the catalyst.

Since life is a series of choices, we can choose to change or remain static. Well-being is a choice. Addictive behavior is a choice. Change is a choice.

And remember, nothing is ever accomplished alone. God compensates for human weakness by providing His strength—the strength needed for addiction-free living.

Questions for discussion:

Who were your lie-tellers?

Were they victims like you?

What are the lies (excess baggage) you carry with you?

What is the level of pain/anger you are feeling now?

Can you commit to change in order to feel better?

What has to happen before you're ready to commit to change?

Room for Thoughts

Chapter 13

* * *

15 Potentially Life-Changing Suggestions (Or: Choosing Life)

1. Commitment to Life

You feel acutely alone, yet you've always felt alone, with no one to talk with or turn to for comfort, no one who understands, no one to trust. The familiar escape route has been blocked, the hiding place lost, and there's no going back. Although temptation remains, the fear of continuing addiction is stronger. Survival is stronger. The need for change is stronger.

There is no need to shout it from the rooftop. No need for group proclamation.

You know you are afflicted with addiction; those around you know. God knows. And that's enough. You've suffered enough humiliation.

Yet, addiction must be acknowledged. Denial is over. The truth must be verbalized for your ears and God's. He hears when the world seems too busy to listen and no one seems to care. He hears the heart-truth. And with compassion and love, He answers.

I suffer from addiction. Addiction is destroying my life. I can no longer nor do I want to live this way. But I am too weak to fight alone and need the strength of One stronger than myself. I need Your help, God. I need Your strength.

Speak from the heart for He hears heart-spoken words.

Raise your hands to receive His support. Surrender to His strength and bask in His unconditional love. Feel that love surround you like a mantle and then praise and thank Him. And NEVER stop.

God will forgive you, so forgive yourself. Good people are addicts. Addiction, not you, bears the responsibility for creating misery. It is the addiction that captures and destroys lives. Not the addict.

Addiction is no longer the god of choice. It is a false god that thrives on evil and lies. Its promises are worthless, born of hatred, not love. Our well-being is not its desire, only our ruin.

Accept your helplessness. Feel and relish the helplessness and then thank God for this helplessness, for it has brought you to Him.

Journal exercise: Rate the first two responses on a scale from 1 (lowest) to 10 (highest).
• What is the amount of pain already suffered due to addiction?
• How much additional pain are you willing to endure?
Decide what needs to happen now. If nothing, admit that and write in sentence form the ultimate outcome of your addiction. The decision is yours alone to make.

What will it take to become sick and tired of feeling sick and tired?

2. Revisit the Past

It is time to pick up your excess baggage and journey into the past. That is where the key is hidden. And when the key is found, you can unpack and return the undeserved articles (the addictive lies) to the rightful owners. The suitcase was packed with articles belonging to another. You don't want them and you're tired of dragging around another's excess baggage.

Addiction hid the key and buried it in despair. Immobilized by hopelessness, you were trapped in a situation without beginning or end. And the exit door was unmarked.

Addiction is a lonely, shame-filled pursuit intended to cauterize wounds gathered in early childhood, but only adds to the trauma, to the depressing weight of the suitcase by amplifying loneliness and shame.

Present and past negativity combine to enslave the addict in a continuum of addiction. And there appears to be no way out. It thrives on negativity, which in turn feeds the addiction. It is cyclical, with no beginning or visible end, and like allies, the past and present unite to perpetuate the lies separating us from the truth.

So, what is the truth hidden beneath the lies? What is the truth so capably camouflaged by addiction?

Please listen with an open heart to the words of Henri J.M. Nouwen in his book *Life of the Beloved:*

> "I have called you by name, from the very beginning" (long before you were wounded by others). "You are mine and I am yours. You

are My Beloved, on you My favor rests…I have carved you in the palms of My hands and hidden you in the shadow of My embrace. I look at you with infinite tenderness and care for you with a care more intimate than that of a mother for her child. I have counted every hair on your head…Wherever you go, I go with you, and wherever you rest, I keep watch…Nothing will ever separate us. We are one."
—In Nouwen's book *Life of the Beloved* p. 36. Crossroad Pub. Co., NY 1992

This is the truth hidden beneath the lies. Read and believe, for you are not just loved, but dearly loved even before your existence. What powerful words. What a powerful proclamation of love.

Why is this so difficult to believe? Why do we listen to everything and everyone except God's truth? Why do we refuse to hear the voice speaking from the core of our existence—our hearts—where the truth resides? Why do we need others-justification to feel love-worthy?

And still the Gentle Voice is not heard.

"I have called you by name from the very beginning." God knows you. He created you out of love. He is strength to our weakness.

"I will not hide my face from you…wherever you are I will be." Just reach out. That's all that's necessary. Reach out in weakness; His hand is waiting.

"Nothing will ever separate us. We are one." No matter what we do, His love is unconditional as He patiently awaits our return.

The truth is: You are God's Beloved child.
You are worthy of His love, peace, and joy.
You cannot overcome addiction without His strength.
He is hope for the hopeless. He is strength for the weak.
As heir, you've inherited God's goodness and beauty.
Since you are His creation, you have God-worth.
You are lovable and worthy of being loved.
Addiction is evil, the addict is not. Addiction deserves the attached feelings of guilt and shame—the addict does not.
Addiction manifests as a psychological dependency upon feel-good substances as a means for balance restoration.
Addiction is hopelessness. God is hope, so reach out in trust—His hand is waiting. You cannot fight addiction without hope-filled love—without the love of the Divine.

Dan Schutte's hymn "Holy Darkness" beautifully expresses this theme of hope:
"I have tried you in the fires of affliction; I have taught your soul to

grieve. In the barren soil of your loneliness, there I will plant my seed. In your deepest hour of darkness I will give you wealth untold...Though My love can seem like a raging storm, this is the love that saves...Were you there when I raised up the mountains? Can you guide the morning star? Does the hawk take flight when you give command? Why do you doubt my power?"

Self-rejection is our greatest enemy because it contradicts the sacred voice calling us "Beloved."

Why do we continue to doubt His power?

* * *

Now let's open the suitcase. Let's find the key and test your commitment to life.

The journey begins by putting on the shoes of a child. Feel the presence of that wide-eyed child as you return to the past. What do you see? How do you feel? Who is there with you? A parent? A caregiver? What's happening?

You need to trace the addictive lies that drove you into the embrace of addiction back to their source; the lies that, like the addiction, restrict emotional development. The lies that inhibit God-given potential.

Wearing your childhood shoes, step into the past and permit your mind the freedom to freely roam. Do not avoid memories because of unpleasantness or fear. Recall all that you can.

Identify feelings of the "not enoughs" lurking within your heart. When and where did these feelings originate? Trace them back to a person(s) or event(s)? What happened? What was said? What was done? How did you feel? Was the other-judgment justified? Was is it true? Decide.

• You feel guilt. Where did the guilt originate? Trace it back. Is it justified?
• You feel shame. Again, decide its origin and justification.
• Continue sorting through emerging feelings.

Journal the information uncovered and compare your newly discovered reality/truth with the addictive lies told by others. Now you can begin to understand where and how your woundedness began.

As children, we depend upon others to judge and anchor our truth, but truth is subjective, based upon biased interpretation. Individual truth is experiential, determined by situations and other-reactions. Individual truth is flawed, for it is not God's truth, but an imperfect version as seen through the imperfect eyes of humanity.

As children, we learn our identity through biased information transmitted either intentionally or unintentionally by parents and caregivers. Fear instilled by a raised hand or harsh word inhibits developmental trust (self and others) and affirmation (self- and others-goodness). Rejection affects our sense of love-worth. Criticism affects our sense of worthiness. Silence creates aloneness. And disappointment, not living up to others-expectation, instills the guilt and shame of the 'not enoughs.'

Negativity, contrary to our innate God-given goodness, creates internal heart-conflict. As God's creation, the heart knows its worth, yet weakened by the external pressure of negative bombardment, succumbs to the mind's acceptance of the reality of abuse. if I am mistreated, I must deserve it—I must be bad.

Children, unable to understand or express their feelings, internalize negative treatment, which resurfaces to influence future relationships and attitudes.

We tend to be critical of what is most feared in ourselves and project these undesirable traits or perceived limitations upon others. Parents, for example, insecure with their own achievements and/or intellect (resulting from the belief in their own addictive lies), may be overly critical of their children's achievements and intelligence.

* * *

Now that you understand your God-worth and have revisited the past to uncover the addictive lies, you can begin to unpack and return those lies to the rightful owners.

Deuteronomy states that the sins of the parents befall the children. Since our self-worth is mirrored in parental eyes, shame and guilt-filled parents will raise shame and guilt-filled children.

Parents have expectations for their children. Some realistic, some more fanciful, yet each generation maintains a similar hope—that each succeeding generation will have more and accomplish more.

Children are natural pleasers and will—in order to gain love and approval—attempt to live up to parental ideals. But, if expectations end in failure and overt parental disappointment, the child feels unworthy.

Being human, failure happens. Although unpleasant, when used as a learning tool, failure provides opportunities for positive growth. But if failure is not an option, if it is not "ok" to make mistakes, self-worth is diminished. And low self-worth escalates into self-hatred, further restricting growth. Present and future opportunities are avoided for fear of additional failure, disapproval, and disappointment.

Facial expressions, words spoken or left unspoken, eloquently diminish self-worth. Disappointment is the silent, unholy halo that settles on our shoulders to weigh us down.

I always hoped for a father-daughter relationship based on mutual love and respect. So I invited my father to attend my doctoral graduation ceremony to be held at Pittsburgh's Civic Arena, thinking that the occasion might develop a bonding. His reply, "I'll be there if I can." Well—he couldn't.

The "what-could-have-beens" are often more painful than the "what was" in life. The possibilities of "what could-have-been" fill us with regret as we ask, "Why couldn't you love and accept me for who I am?"

The answer is simple, "Because you did not know me."

For many years I bitterly regretted the time lost with my parents. The 'what-could-have-beens' and in my mind the "what-should-have-beens." Like an old record, these thoughts replayed ending in profound disappointment—not anger, just disappointment. I dreamed, I wished things could have been different, but they weren't—a fact that I eventually had to admit and accept. There was no storybook ending, no tear-felt apologies. Nothing.

They did not know me—nor I them.

3. Forgiveness Comes with Opening the Suitcase.

Forgiveness of self and others is essential to well-being for balancing mind, body, and heart.

God forgives and so must we. But it is not easy to forgive those who have wounded us, those who have miss-shaped our identity. At times our minds scream out with the injustice of our wounding, as if wounds were one-sided. But they are not, for only the wounded can inflict wounds.

So, what can we do when the pain is too great to forgive?

Love is the answer. And since God is love, we turn to Him for curative love, which soothes pain and renews the heart. So turn to God for He is the Master of forgiveness. Go to Him in the rawness of pain and profess your inability to release and forgive those held responsible; confess your inability to let go of the anger and disappointment that plagues your heart and tortures your mind. Confess your weakness and plead for His strength.

Ask for self-forgiveness. And receive His forgiveness. Bask in His forgiveness, allowing it to release the hurt as lightness enters your heart.

Allow yourself to accept His unconditional love and transfer that love to those who have injured you. Visualize the love. Allow it to seep from you into them. Let it ooze from your heart in understanding and compassion. And allow yourself to forgive as God has forgiven.

Know that as a child you were blameless. You did nothing to deserve anything but unconditional love from those around you. That is your birthright as God's Beloved.

Now open the suitcase and sort through its contents. See the guilt, pick it up, examine it, and decide whether it rightly belongs to you or to another. If not your possession, replace the guilt within the suitcase.

See the shame? Can you claim responsibility? If not, after examination replace it within the suitcase. Continue to inspect all the negative feelings, feelings of worthlessness, self-doubt, and lovelessness. And either remove or retain them within the suitcase.

Lock the suitcase when all the items have been delegated to their rightful owners. And realize you are now in control for you possess the key—the truth—your truth hidden since childhood when you were forced to carry another's burden.

Since the suitcase and its contents no longer belong to you, the negativity and lies contained within need to be properly disposed. It would be inappropriate to dismiss the suitcase as unimportant, for its contents are as real as its former influence over your life.

It's time to return the suitcase to its rightful owner for it doesn't belong to you and never has. You were carrying it for someone else. And now, with love and understanding, you will return the excess baggage that has caused so much suffering.

For this process, here are two suggestions—be creative as you mentally unlock the suitcase for a second time:

Write all the negative feelings and emotions contained within the suitcase on slips of paper, along with specific scenarios. Affix these papers, using glue or rubber bands, to bricks or rocks, and place them in a real suitcase. Lock it. Lift the suitcase and feel its weight—feel the weight in your hand as it travels up your arm and into your shoulder. This is the burden your heart has carried since childhood. Carry the suitcase, visibly straining under the weight, and either deliver it to its rightful owner along with your forgiveness (they are victims too), well-wishes, and gratitude to God, or dispose of it on garbage day.

Or, express your feelings in a letter. Write quickly whatever enters your mind without stopping to edit. Let the feelings flow without censor. It will be your choice whether or not to mail the letter. You might burn the letter outdoors and watch all the pain-filled lies disappear into the heavens.

I chose the letter approach.

Dearest Mums,
You are my mother. I love you and I always will.
Even though I remind myself that the past has passed, it sometimes haunts my mind and heart. Even though I am well into my adult years, the residue of negative childhood memories continues to affect my behavior and attitudes.
I remember the volatility of our family structure, never knowing when but certain that an emotional explosion was imminent. I was scared and guilt-ridden knowing I was the cause.
I thought perhaps if I behaved better, if I wasn't always sick, or if I was invisible, you wouldn't always be angry.
I blamed myself.
At the time I did not understand that the anger would have existed with or without my

presence. You were hurting, I know that now. And your hurt, hurt me.

Your unhappiness affected me. Your frustration affected me. Your anger affected me.

I now understand that the relationship between you and your husband was addictive. Your behavior was addictive for you fed off each other as addict and enabler. Your behavior negatively affected the family. With or without your awareness this behavior had a detrimental effect on all our lives.

As I write this letter I feel sadness for what was and what could have been—emotions I must release for my own well-being.

I also release you, my dearest Mums, for you are my mother and I will always love you. And I forgive you, for you were a victim, too.

Mariah

Dear Lou,

A love-hate relationship exists between us. You were never satisfied. Nothing ever seemed to please you—certainly not me.

I feared you. I hated you. Yet, I loved you. A love you were incapable of returning.

I pity you and your pathetic, solitary life. Out of pity I am able to release you, for you, too, were a victim of the addictive lies. I give you my pity and forgiveness.

Mariah

4. Introduce Yourself

Since the lie-tellers were mistaken, it's time for an introduction. By projecting their fears and weaknesses upon you, you were created in their image without knowledge or regard for your God-given uniqueness. As another's design, your internal truth never emerged.

Your parents or caregivers do not know you and it's time for an introduction. Again, this is just a suggestion which can be customized.

Establish time for a mutually convenient meeting and begin with a handshake. (You might present a business card with name and title, ie. John: God's Beloved.) Remember, your mission is not one of confrontation or apology. As with any job interview, verbalize your mission, your statement of objective. For example: "I want to develop an honest relationship based on mutual love, honesty, and respect."

Express your love and acknowledge, but do not apologize for, your addiction, the cross born out of desperation, the cross of negativity and despair.

Or, you might chose to put your introduction into letter form, with an option to mail it or release it into the heavens.

Example:

We've met, but you don't know me. Let me introduce myself. I am…(list attributes). Just like you, I am one of God's creations and as such I am loved and lovable. I am not perfect and was never intended to be. I make mistakes, I learn from these mistakes, and I don't make them again. I am worthy in the eyes of God and in my own eyes. My worth is not determined by any human. My limitations will no longer be determined by another and I will soar with God's grace to be the person I was meant to be. And I will walk each day hand in hand with my Creator. I will do all I humanly can and leave the rest to God.

I have not come to argue or cast blame. What I am doing, I am doing for myself. You may agree or not, but I'm not seeking your approval for I approve of myself. And I am OK.

If the lie-tellers are unwilling to listen or are intent on confrontation, end the meeting. By arguing, the advantage is lost, putting you on the defensive. Leave because you understand—you've changed and they have not. You know the truth while they still suffer from the lies told them.

Wish them well, content in the knowledge that you have been released from the negativity that controlled and hampered your life. Leave with the freedom of one residing in the light of truth.

* * *

Your past no longer controls the present or limits the future. With the hope and trust of one of God's Beloved, expect His limitless goodness. Faith and the power of love are the only two essentials in life. Nothing else is needed.

And pass it on. This truth is too good not to share, this life-giving, restorative message. Live as you were intended to live—free of addiction and free of addictive lies. **And praise God for He is good. Life is good.**

5. *Change Your Environment*

Change environments and end relationships that are conducive to or associated with abuse. Like addiction, former places and relationships are toxic. You've journeyed this far, and with God's help, your journey will continue.

Seek healthy and positive individuals, passionate for life and living. Reenter society by joining purposeful groups committed to inspiring love and hope.

Return to school or get a job to break addiction's cycle of self-containment for idle/alone time is dangerous. **Boredom is dangerous.**

Find a hobby or pursue a passion sidestepped because of abuse. Be creative. Allow yourself to dream, and then follow that dream for anything is possible.

Now that mind and heart are approaching balance, work on the body. Exercise. Ride a bike or locate those long forgotten rollerblades and enjoy the thrill of physical freedom.

Read for improvement or pleasure. Join a book club and share mind-broadening ideas.

If you reach out in love, others will reach back. Open your heart to love and it will be filled. Give it a try. It feels good to not be alone. **Rejoice in humanity, for it rejoices in you.**

6. Be Thankful

Looking through the eyes of love, a joy-filled heart sees beauty in the ordinary. It thrills to the perfection in a flower. It swoons at the magnificence of a bird soaring through the sky. It sees the face of God in every man. And it gives thanks for life's goodness.

The accepting mind resides in the knowledge of its well-being. At peace, it no longer suffers the exhaustion of attempted control and prefers God's will above its own. No longer bombarded by negative thoughts, it is freed to exercise its potential. And it gives thanks.

The healthy body is respectful of itself. Viewed as God's creation, it is properly nourished and exercised for maximum functioning. In its radiant well-being it gives thanks to God.

Recently, I called a cleaning company with the sole intention of saying "thank you" for a job well done. The receptionist was so amazed that she immediately transferred the call to the owner, stating he needed to hear something positive, something other than a complaint.

As a society, we don't say "thank you" nearly enough. Why is it easier to complain than to say 'thank you?'

God is bombarded with complaints as we tell Him our wants and expectations. I doubt if He is bombarded with heartfelt "thank yous." Try just one day of gratitude without complaining. And then try another.

Be thankful for a new beginning, a life free of abuse. Begin each day with gratitude, committing to remain addiction-free one day at a time. And rejoice at day's end.

Be aware of your surroundings and thankful for daily goodnesses regardless of their seeming insignificance. Acknowledge the source of that goodness and give thanks.

Thank God for the freedom to live and love as you were intended.

Saying "thank you" is an acknowledgement of appreciation. And even God wants to be appreciated.

7. Give of Yourself

As humans, we are not solitary beings. Man was placed on earth to be of service to one another, which implies the risk of rejection as we offer ourselves in love. When we reach out in love, it allows another the privilege of reaching back in love. Sharing of oneself is the greatest expression of human love.

The addict's world is created for the sole survival and perpetuation of the addiction. Break the mold and escape. Take a chance that will lead to change.

Like snowflakes, no two individuals are alike. Think about the limitless human potential. Think about the new discoveries—challenging and validating existence—just waiting for you to reach out and take a chance.

For most individuals change is possible. For the addict, change is not only possible but necessary for survival with God's help. **He has brought you this far and He will not abandon you now.**

Trust in God and trust in yourself. Trust in the many wonders you have been given to share. We are not solitary beings, so freely extend yourself to others. Give and receive without expectations, for sharing is an act of selflessness.

My mother, after my first divorce and annulment, decided to stay with me for a few months, which stretched into many years. So under the guise of assisting me, she essentially separated from her husband.

She became the mother I needed and the grandmother my children adored. Stricken with cancer, she died in my arms—just the two of us, together. Alone—as it was meant to be.

My father died as alone as he lived.

8. What Is Life's Purpose?

Entangled within the arms of abuse, life had but one purpose—to perpetuate the addiction. The daily pursuit of addiction was our only thought. But, once released, life becomes purpose-filled. There is a reason, a meaning for every speck, for every cell of life, seen and unseen, in existence. There is a reason for each and every member of mankind.

Addiction is not a life-purpose, for it restricts personal and emotional growth. It denies exploration and discovery of who we are and what we were intended to become.

We are the sum product of our total experiences based upon our interpretation of the experiences, which can either stunt our growth or propel us beyond our imaginings.

Each roadblock or speed bump encountered provides the potential for growth and a clue, for the observant interpreter, as to life's purpose. When viewed as opportunities for change, the mind and heart open to God's intention. When we decipher the clues that satisfy the heart, we find purpose.

The answer is within. Just listen to your heart.

9. Be Thankful Some More

Express gratitude for whatever happens. It is easy to be grateful for the goodness in life, but difficult to say "thank you" for life's unpleasantness. Remember, God is not the source of evil. He is the constant love evidenced in all circumstances—if we look. So, be thankful and cling to that love. Express gratitude for addiction, for it provided the opportunity to become a seeker of truth. **And be grateful, for truth bestows freedom.**

10. Continue Daily Journaling

Journal changing thoughts, hopes, and fears. Write about potential opportunities and your intention in turning these opportunities into vehicles of change. Write about your dreams, those derailed due to abuse, and plan how to now pursue these dreams. List the pros and cons of addiction. What have you gained? What has it cost you? And weigh the results.

Plant dream seeds in your heart, nurture them daily, and watch them grow.

11. Future Hopes

List your goals. Determine concrete steps to be taken today, tomorrow, next week, and beyond. in order to attain those goals. By now you are aware of strengths and limitations, so the goal setting should be fairly accurate. And decide to do something every day that will take you closer to your goals. Record your progress. And adjust as required.

12. Moments of Weakness

There will be moments of weakness, so expect them. Times when addiction appears without blemish and extremely appealing; when the insidious temptation seems too much to bear. You know it's coming, for you sense its nearness in the increased agitation of mind and body.

You feel alone, isolated from the world, and all that exists is you and the escalating temptation. Resolve slips as your mind considers abdicating control to the gods of addiction, the gods of compelling lies.

Evil masquerades as goodness as perspectives change and the ability to choose waivers, the false-gods beckon you by name.

But must you succumb in defeat to the enemy? Must you submit to the enticement of a false lover? Must you nestle into the waiting arms of addiction?

God rains upon everyone alike—the good, the bad, the privileged, the poverty-stricken. You have not been singled out, for everyone suffers in life.

When life becomes too hard to stand, kneel. Kneel and thank God for His goodness. Confide your feelings and fears; He understands. Admit your weakness and ask for His strength. Place the addiction at His feet, for you can no longer handle it. You don't want it. Place yourself in His capable hands. And believing in His assistance, give thanks.

Don't be alone. Have a predetermined "safe place" to go to that feeds and refreshes mind, body, and heart; a place where others need and appreciate your uniqueness. Give of yourself and, in giving, allow God to return.

Exercise. Walk. Run. Do anything physically strenuous to counteract the abusive urge until it subsides and you regain balance.

Review what addiction jeopardizes—what you have to lose. And decide if it is worth it.

Put your feelings into words; list your physical symptoms, the emotional draw of addiction. Romanticize the addiction as a lover, how it makes you feel, think, and behave. Recall the good times together and then watch your lover change into an evil beast waiting to prey upon your defenselessness. With claws dripping blood and fangs glistening with the intent to devour, the beast (Satan) mounts its attacks. He wants you to fail. **God wants you to succeed.**

Retrace your journey to recovery. Go back to the beginning and retrace the steps, the progress made. You've come a long way, so be proud. Remember your goals, feel and luxuriate in the pride of anticipated accomplishment when these goals are achieved. Think positively; your life depends upon it.

Keep a constant reminder, concrete evidence of the consequences of addiction, always present and within reach. Something tangible representing what you fear the most, physical actions or losses resulting as consequences of addiction.

Mine is the wrist band worn in detox. It's hung like Christ on the cross in my room. (I most fear the loss of freedom.)

List all that you are grateful for, no matter how insignificant, and bask in gratitude while recognizing the source of the goodness. **And remember to CONSTANTLY say "THANK YOU."**

13. Additional Journal Entries
Since each day presents roadblocks, be prepared by devising strategies to handle these unforeseen challenges, life's unexpected events. Determine how you will/will not react; how you will handle the unforeseen—the life-surprises.

Revise and fine tune strategies. And turn to God, for He is your greatest fan.

14. Rewards
Think of a safe reward. And reward yourself occasionally. You deserve it for surviving addiction.

15. Adopt an "I Can Do It" Attitude
Anything is possible with the love of God—including surviving addiction. **Positive thinking leads to positive actions.**

Questions for discussion:
So, what do you think?

Is this doable?

Will you try?

Room for Thoughts

Part Three

Chapter 14

* * *

Love and Respect

During my undergraduate studies at Hofstra University, flaunting nineteen years of life experience, I wrote a descriptive article entitled "Love." After stating within the first paragraph that love was indefinable, I proceeded for the next four pages to define a word requiring a lifetime's understanding which I did not possess.

I have since decided that age and experience define love while the imaginary love of my youth was based on romantic book and movie images. Along with eyesight, those images have faded as love became the foundation of all life-interaction. It is love's stability that I depend upon, knowing that it's always there to keep me going when I would rather not.

When a smile stretches your mouth from ear to ear at the mere thought of a love object— that is love. It's more than a feeling. It's a knowing that I am loved unconditionally with all my flaws and inconsistencies. And regardless of mistakes, I will remain loved and always be forgiven.

Love is not ownership or expectation. It is eternal if both parties are willing. It is soft, yet at times blares with the intensity of a Sousa March. Yes, I love love and the closeness and dependency upon my loved one for the continuous sharing of goodness.

Yet, when I surrendered myself to love, giving all that I am—the good, the bad, and all that dwells in between— to another, I am not depleted, but rather filled. Because of love, my purpose is to selflessly please another— a thought foreign to my youthful mind, for then I believed love was to please me.

To give of yourself without expectation of return, that is love. It is a selfless act that satisfies as nothing else. Selflessness is love.

It seems appropriate to restate a story about my favorite couple who are so obviously in love. I asked, "What's your secret?"

His smile was sweet as he answered, quickly and without thought, for he knew the answer. "My purpose is to help her to become the best she can be."

Wow! Now, isn't that also God's purpose?

* * *

Love is not possible without respecting the living. I believe that society's greatest problem is the lack of respect for life.

Abortion, euthanasia, all killings are the ultimate sign of disrespect regardless of intent or intellectualization. Although beyond human creation, life is not beyond human extinction.

Disrespect prevails at all age levels and within all social settings. Consider student bullying in today's schools—acts that can and do lead to teen suicide and deaths. How can that be when we are equalized by the same life force?

Gang violence, rape, and wars are all grounded in disrespect, which objectifies and dehumanizes its victims.

Anger and physical and mental abuse are based in disrespect. How can we hold each other in such low esteem when God, by His love, has raised us so high?

We don't respect others, for we don't respect ourselves.

Questions for discussion:

How do you define love?

How does it feel to be loved? To love others?

Have you ever been the target of a bully? Have you ever bullied others?

How does it feel?

What can you do about it?

Room for Thoughts

Chapter 15

* * *

Mourn the Loss

It's time to mourn the loss of addiction. Like most life-losses, it is necessary to allow yourself time to work through the grief process from initial denial to acceptance.

Acceptance of addiction is difficult for we don't want to be different. We don't want to be singled out as possessing weaknesses in areas most individuals successfully participate in at varying levels.

It is a personal affront to our sense of freewill to admit loss of control. It is difficult to accept our inability to "party" on the weekends with friends. Or to count calories when others carelessly eat whatever looks pleasing.

It is difficult to ignore gratifying memories when our former lover appears bearing flowers and promises of better days. It is easy to lie to ourselves by reassigning responsibility or blaming others. It is easy to judge and compare "worse" addictions and deem ourselves not so bad off. After all, we only drink wine while they consume bourbon and vodka. We only snort while they inject abusive substances. It is easy to deny addiction's iron grasp by believing that we can heal alone.

It is difficult to ignore memories of the addictive pleasures replaying in our minds. The exaggerated scenarios as addiction overcomes life's wrongs while bypassing the inevitable consequences as mindless as puffs of smoke in the air.

Addiction is a solitary pursuit. The healing process, on the other hand, requires reaching out to others while presenting them with opportunity to reach back in understanding and love.

We must view addiction for what it is—an evil liar and a destroyer of lives. So mourn as you would any loss from denial to acceptance. And then know that you are free, for the loss of addiction means freedom. So bask in your newly gained freedom and be thankful.

Questions for discussion:

Recall a significant life-loss. How did you feel? Discuss your phases of mourning.

Did you receive help through the process? Who or what helped?

Did it make a difference?

Could you have done it alone?

Room for Thoughts

Chapter 16

* * *

Nutrition and Addiction

Nutrition can aid in remaining addiction-free. If we think of the brain as a computer, this makes sense. If the battery is low or you forget to press the power key, it won't function (Computer 101).

Chemical messengers or neurotransmitters (synapses) must run at peak performance for the information in the brain to be processed correctly. Serotonin, endorphins, GABA, and dopamine are neurotransmitters that handle all communications relating to emotional well-being and tranquility.

When the neurotransmitters or synapses function improperly, transmission is garbled, and we begin to feel intense loneliness, stress, anxiety, and depression.

All drug and alcohol addicts suffer from malnutrition. It's interesting that only fat contains more calories per gram than alcohol. So, when drinking, addicts experience a sense of fullness after eating little or nothing. These empty calories lead to poor eating habits and malnutrition. Drug abusers experience a similar effect. Alcohol and drugs prevent the body from properly absorbing and breaking down nutrients and expelling toxins.

Malnutrition only exacerbates the feelings of tension and general malaise the addict was attempting to avoid. This then becomes another vicious circle for the addict never actually feels well anymore.

If the addict started feeling well again, all cravings for abusive substances could eventually be erased and he would be freed to refocus and redirect his life in a positive direction.

Since amino acids are the stuff neurotransmitters are composed of, it makes sense to supply the body with an abundance of specific amino acids to restore functioning, reduce cravings, and restore one's sense of well-being while reducing the possibility of relapse. Every newly recovering addict struggles with cravings to use alcohol and drugs. Research has shown that a diet with the right types of high protein such as meat and dairy products, fish, beans, leafy vegetables, and nuts and seeds and high carbohydrate-rich foods can make a big deference.

Whole foods (those without preservatives or additives, nonprocessed foods) aid not only the addict but should be incorporated into all of our lives. They are the basic foods, the natural foods that remain untampered with by manufacturers who seem to take pride in removing all that is naturally good and replacing it with artificiality.

Select fruits and vegetables from the fruit and vegetable department, uncontaminated meat, poultry, and fish from whole food markets. Selectively choose processed foods with the least amount of ingredients and additives. For example, rice should contain only one ingredient—rice. And a box of oatmeal—only oatmeal.

The body craves carbohydrates when it is lacking other vital nutrients. So, replace sugar and refined starches with fresh fruit and whole grains to help restore balance.

It is better to eat small, frequent mini-meals to maintain energy levels and moods more evenly. Eat three meals and three snacks per day. Drink decaffeinated coffee and tea to decrease the intake of caffeine. Be aware of hidden sugar in cocoa, condiments, and over-the-counter medications. Be aware of caffeine in over-the-counter and prescription medications.

Multiple vitamin/mineral supplements should be taken because drugs and alcohol deplete the body of needed vitamins and minerals. Vitamins and dietary supplements should be taken with meals to assure optimum absorption.

Exercise and Addiction

The essence of recovery is changing negative behaviors into positive behaviors. Good nutrition along with exercise and relaxation play an important role in successful change.

Exercise, like all things in life, should be done in moderation. It should be consistent and frequent—four times a week for at least one hour per session.

Exercise:
- increases the metabolic rate so that calories are efficiently burned even at rest
- burns stored fat and builds muscle tissue; muscles burn calories and are metabolically active whereas fat cells are inert
- increases free fatty acids, which better aids the body in processing and utilizing dietary fats
- decreases total serum cholesterol and increases the "good fats" associated with lowering the risk of heart attacks
- lowers blood pressure
- increases the level of mood-elevating neurochemicals such as endorphins, so that

we feel better mentally as well as physically

Aerobic exercises such as walking, jogging, and cycling cause the body to use large amounts of oxygen and burn calories. Anaerobic exercises such as weight training and calisthenics develop muscular strength and flexibility without increasing the pulse or heart rate.

Tips: choose an activity you like; choose a convenient location; start slowly; dress appropriately; listen to your body's cues; and stick with it.

Meditation and Relaxation Techniques

There are times we need to stop the racing of our minds, the nonstop thoughts that constrict our chests with labored breathing. It would be wonderful to stop or at least slow these unnerving thoughts that threaten our well-being and restore interior calm. At times the thought of just not thinking seems to be the most blessed thought of all.

Relaxation brings immediate relief to muscle tension, calms breathing, and slows brain activity. And we are at peace. In this relaxed state the hard edges of reality soften and appear less and less important. As we breathe slowly and deeply, shoulder and neck muscles relax and the mind is freed to wander or not think at all.

This sensation is similar to the sensation of addiction, but with no addictive and harmful side effects. Meditation or relaxation techniques are not harmful because our minds do this naturally when not in active use.

It is a useful technique when the urge to use drugs threatens to overtake the resolve not to. It provides distraction, a source of focus at times of weakness. Meditation costs nothing, it's always available, and most importantly, it puts us back in control of ourselves.

Deep breathing—a quick, deep breath in through the nose, using the diaphragm, followed by a long, extended exhale through the mouth. Repeat until feeling calmer. Be aware of your breath. Focus on one area of the body; you might start with the head and work downward, releasing the tension with each outward breath.

Visualization—find the center of your cravings. See the size and shape and draw a line around the edges. Don't hurry. Remain with this image for a while. Don't push it away. Let it be, and when the time is right (you will know) let it go.

Or see yourself at the top of a staircase. You will slowly descend, taking one step at a time. With each step allow body and mind to relax more and more until the landing is reached, at which time you feel totally relaxed.

Or picture yourself at the beach or some favorite place where you relax. Smell, feel, and see what is around you. Become part of that place and relax.

*Soothing music and rhythmic sounds—your breathing, heart, and mind (personal rhythms) will slow to the rhythm of repetitive sound such as music or water or bells or the repetition of a phrase or word.

These are just several of many relaxation techniques available. Remember that well-being requires a three-pronged effort—that of mind, body, and heart.

Questions for discussion:

Keep a food log. Rate your eating habits—times and food choices. How can you improve?

Did you exercise prior to addiction? If not, are you willing to start?

When?

Today?

Chapter 17

* * *

Oblivion

Occasionally it would be nice to slip back into oblivion, into the waiting arms of nothingness. It would be easy to reassume the role of nonexistence when the world demands our full energy and attention. At times, it is easier to escape than face new and change-provoking situations.

Since addiction is a learned behavior, what has been learned can be unlearned. There are healthy ways of problem solving and, unlike addiction, these solutions bear little or no consequences.

At times life is boring, a frustrating scenario of "hurry up and wait." Hurry up and do your part and then sit back and wait for something to happen, outcomes determined by others.

Rarely are directional signs planted along life's highway stating when to turn to avoid the bumps and roadblocks. Rarely do signs appear recommending options.

But wouldn't it be nice to know whether to choose option #1 or option #2?

Unfortunately, life doesn't happen that way. No one sails through life without a scratch. We are all scratched and dented—battle-scarred. But guess what? It is the bruises and scars that make us who we are. It is the things that happen to us that make our stories worth telling.

We have freedom of choice to interpret situations. We are free to positively or negatively adjust our lives according to that interpretation or to remain static.

And if we decide to remain static and are unwilling to change? Have you ever noticed reoccurring life problems and wondered why these concerns reappear with continuing regularity?

Problems and roadblocks are training devices providing the lessons needed to be learned in order to become the individuals we are intended to be. Some people never learn and remain in a lifetime of arrested development, continually complaining of the same personal or work-related issues while others discover the joy of fulfillment.

Open your eyes and heart for the truth is before you. Only when the crutch of addictive behavior is removed can God reveal His unique plan for our lives. So, throw away the crutch and enjoy God's limitless power.

Walk with God. He will teach you. Listen and He will speak. Meet Him in spite of opposition and He will reveal His will.

Life is a school. Learn from it.

I have learned that my addiction was born out of a need to hurt others. If I felt neglected, unloved, or unappreciated I would punish the offenders by drinking. Regardless of my suffering, they suffered too—I returned hurt for hurt. Instead of acknowledging and verbalizing the hurt, I childishly struck out in retaliation for some slight my parents, family, or acquaintances may or may not have been aware of.

Drinking may have accomplished my goal, attempting to control others, but was far outweighed by the consequences.

Instead of discovering the real me with all my glorious strengths and weaknesses, I chose to blame others for my actions—they caused my unhappiness, they caused my drinking.

Now I realize the ridiculousness of these statements. And accept complete responsibility for my behavior.

* * *

There is a point in time (no matter how brief) when the need/desire to stop overrides the addiction. A moment in time when control shifts.

There is a window of opportunity that presents itself as the effects of the substance declines—a kind of "no-man's-land" or neutral territory that evens the players as clarity of mind returns. And quite unexpectedly, the haze of oblivion lifts.

It's like switching on the light in a darkened room, allowing the familiar to become real. Or awakening from a deep sleep without memory, only the reality of the present.

It is during this period that addiction abdicates control. It is during this period, before the physical symptoms of withdrawal set in, that we have a choice.

This brief window of opportunity closes with the onset of withdrawal—physical discomfort that gets worse before it gets better—before thoughts of re-cocooning into oblivion regain appeal. But by then it's too late, for the opportunity has been lost and addiction again becomes what it is—a delaying tactic.

It requires strength and courage to suffer. And isn't addiction the avoidance of (emotional) suffering? And withdrawal (physical) is suffering—both to be avoided by those well-educated in pain avoidance.

"No-man's-land" does exist. And I believe that God is the light in the darkened room. He is there to provide a choice, a new path that leads to Him. He is that brief clarity of thought. He is the strength and courage we lack, although we seek it through addiction.

He is that sudden glaring reality that we are still alive, as the background in which we have been existing becomes the foreground. He created "no-man's-land" as a way to end addiction. As an opportunity to choose Him over addiction, as an opportunity to simply say, "I need You. And Your courage and strength."

"No-man's-land" is God-created for a God-intervention. The reprieve that allows us to choose, a free-will choice between Him and continuing addiction. He will help carry the cross if we ask.

Several questions come to mind: "If this is a God-intervention, why the heck did He did take so long?

And the answer, "He didn't. We did. He was always there."

Which begs the next question, "So then, why did it take us so long?

Remember free will? We must take the first step.

Why does He allow us to stray? Why doesn't He just bop us on the head and tell us to stop behaving so badly?

Simply because that's not His modus operandi. He provides the opportunity that we must recognize and accept.

DEAR LORD, PLEASE DON'T ALLOW THIS WORK FROM YOUR HANDS (ME) BE WASTED.

Feeling Distant From God?

Who moved? It wasn't Him.

He's as stable as the rock of Gibraltar. And His residency never changes.

We are the ones who distance ourselves from God. We remove ourselves emotionally during times of duress and even during happiness. We blame Him for life's hardness and forget to share our joy.

Although we were created in His image, at times our humanity takes forefront. And we see with eyes grounded and focused upon ourselves. Our wants and disappointments overtake feelings of love and gratitude.

The 'I' mentality steps forward to claim our thoughts and erase every goodness God has given us. And all we think about is what we lack. Materialistic things: the vacation house at the beach; that five-bedroom contemporary in an upscale neighborhood; the perfect relationship; the perfect life.

And we feel disappointed, for other people have those things. So, why can't we?

We feel rejection when we are passed over for a promotion.

We feel slighted when that party invitation fails to arrive.

We feel neglected by our friends, spouse, and children who fail to include us into their busy schedules.

We feel betrayed when a confidence is compromised.

We have all experienced these human emotions. We know them too well. But guess what? So, has God. He has been disappointed, rejected, slighted, neglected, and betrayed. By us.

We forget that He has experienced what we experience. He knows hurt and sadness. He knows loneliness.

He understands. The problem is that we do not.

We don't understand that God is our greatest ally, our greatest source of comfort. We prefer to go it alone, enjoying the isolation of our emotional misery.

But we're never alone and life is good if we anchor in the present, not in past "what-could-have-been's" nor future "what-might-be's." We must live in the present for opportunity resides in the present. And happiness and growth are only possible in the present.

But, most importantly, God is in the present, surrounding us with His beauty and goodness to insure that we are never alone. He is the lover and confidant who will never disappoint, reject, slight, neglect, or betray.

He understands.

Questions for discussion:

Have you felt the need for oblivion? Describe the situation.

What did you do?

Can you identify reoccurring problems? What are they?

Since reoccurring problems represent unlearned lessons, what lessons do you need to learn?

Room for Thoughts

Chapter 18

* * *

Why I Drank

I drank because I could, and I didn't like anyone telling me otherwise.

I drank in retaliation (punishment) of perceived neglect or unfair treatment by others. I drank when promises were broken.

I drank to hurt those who hurt me, blaming them and not myself for insobriety.

I drank out of boredom, for no one was providing me entertainment.

I drank because of broken dreams and promises.

I drank because of the "not enoughs". I was never clever enough nor good enough to please my parents. And ultimately—to please myself.

I drank because I didn't know myself.

And I drank to feel better. To feel whole and in balance.

Addictive lies are the catalysts for addiction. Addictive lies set us up for failure by predicting the failure. Disguised as the truth, they handicap potential while detaining us in a stagnant and guilt-ridden existence.

Lies and alcohol are my co-burdens carried simultaneously throughout the years. But, only one was obvious, the one others saw. And I, like them, never looked any deeper.

Alcohol, like any addictive substance, is only the tip of the iceberg, which many recovery programs tend to ignore. They seem more concerned in establishing social clubs, which in addition to providing entertainment and the camaraderie of shared experience, provide a crutch constructed upon human instability instead of human strength.

I did not immediately embrace the Divine, although I acknowledged His existence. For many years we fought for control, He and I. Actually, I was the one fighting while He waited patiently.

I screamed, crying out in my impatience, wanting to be cured. But, placing myself on par with the Master, I had not yet learned my lesson and needed to be humbled.

Humiliation is humbling. Alcoholism is humbling. The consequences of addictive behavior are humbling until we finally admit we have had enough. That day I prayed for forgiveness. I prayed for a God-intervention. And He heard.

Acceptance of our burdens (addictions) lightens the cross. Acceptance of our weakness and dependency upon God lightens our heart.

And what a relief when Someone of such great strength comes to our rescue.

I've realized that addiction (the emotional high associated with a state of wellness) began for me in early childhood.

As a child I suffered from asthma, the debilitating illness affecting one's ability to breathe. I clearly remember the sound and feel as I strained with each constricted breath. Elephants weighing upon my chest as I lay in bed waiting for the medication to ease their presence, anticipating the rush, the blessed release of tension. And it happened night after night, a physical and emotional surge, a high that brought peace and well-being.

This blessed high in later years was recreated in the form of alcohol. Both caused similar feel-good effects—the emotional high of wellness. The transfer was familiar and immediate.

I no longer drink because I no longer want to waste the remainder of my allotted time on earth.

I no longer drink because the reasons for not drinking far outweigh the reasons for drinking.

I no longer drink because life is much more pleasant in a state of sobriety.

I no longer drink because I like the sober me.

I no longer drink because the consequences of drinking are too great.

I no longer drink because I have learned a better way to handle disappointment and neglect.

I no longer drink because I no longer need to blame others. I accept responsibility for my behavior.

I no longer drink because once accepting God's love, I have learned to love and accept myself for who I am minus the addictive lies.

I no longer drink because life is too good to miss.

I no longer drink because God's plan for me does not include addiction.

It is my choice to drink or not to drink. And I chose not to.

Self-discovery is essential in beating addiction. We need to delve beneath the water's surface to reveal the hidden and painful lies. But it is the only way to beat addiction, and with God's help, we will.

Questions for discussion:

You have explored your addictive lies. Are there other factors contributing to addiction? Explain.

Why have you participated in addiction? List reasons.

List reasons for not participating.

Room for Thoughts

Chapter 19

* * *

Thoughts Too Good Not to Share

Truth originates in the heart, and when you speak, people will listen because they recognize heart-truth. When we speak from the heart, we speak with love and God is love. So, when we speak from the heart, we speak God's truth. I believe *Addictive Lies* to be God's truth.

Like water seeking its own level, we sometimes behave in the extreme to feel (to imitate) a sense of well-being and balance. This is addiction—an emotional state.

Anything contained or hoarded within is unhealthy. All we have and all we are is meant to be shared.

Addiction is self-hoarding. It is a protective measure to prevent and avoid pain, yet ultimately causes more suffering.

Hoarders can be cured by releasing that which is hoarded—blame, guilt, rejection. The remaining void must be filled with love.

Addiction is learned behavior. And what is learned can be unlearned.

God created man as a magnificent creature with the ability to change. Change allows growth.

Although there are many types of addiction—food, drugs, alcohol, materialism, acquisitions, etc.—all result from a selfish and ultimately ill-fated pursuit of well-being and balance.

Victims are usually the victims of other victims. It is generational.

Attempted control is exhausting. Pretending to be strong is exhausting. And what a relief it is to rely on Someone of infinite strength.

God's love is unblemished. It accepts us at our best and at our worst. It is a love that asks nothing but to love in return.

I will soar with God's grace to be all that I can. And I am not afraid, for I now walk hand in hand with my Creator.

Allow yourself to love. And allow yourself to be loved.

I can fly higher than an eagle because You are the wind beneath my wings.

Chapter 20

* * *

Praise God

In God-balanced living, the mind discovers that it can rely on Another for strength; that it need not face the world alone; that its willfulness is based not in love but in control. And it gains the freedom "to be" rather than "to do" as control is replaced by acceptance.

The body, viewed as a vessel created by God, is treated with respect. It is not abused by internal or external substances. It is not overfed or neglected. It is physically and emotionally nourished and loved as a gift from God.

The heart is joy-filled for it acknowledges the presence of God in us all. And since God is love, the heart radiates His love. Love permeates our thoughts, words, and actions. Love and positivity is recognized in all people and all situations regardless of initial surface perception.

Mind, body, and heart bask in trust and hope, knowing our beloved-ness. We are God's Beloved creations (not just loved, but much-loved). And as God's Beloved, we are heirs to His goodness and protection.

When the heart, mind, and body interact harmoniously, peace presides over our world regardless of the surrounding peacelessness. We experience a sense of well-being that colors thoughts and behavior. Our attitudes soften and we become more accepting and life becomes easier, for the battle to control has ended. And in that end we find the freedom to simply be the best of who and what we are. Instead of the daily grind, life becomes a daily adventure, filled with God's little surprises. And roadblocks become opportunities or blessings which indicate change instead of mind, body, and heart-numbing dead ends. It's all perception—positivity of thought versus negativity.

God-balance is the ideal functional state. When mind, body, and heart operate harmoniously we are at the top of our game. Although not perfect, life is good and we are able to deal with its imperfections because we are grounded in the Divine.

God is the key. He is the difference between emptiness and joy. Control over situations or acceptance of an intelligence and goodness greater than our own. He is the difference between abusing and respecting our bodies. He is life's purpose. And He is the strength to achieve that purpose.

As His creations, we were meant to be happy. Take a moment to look around. Would He have created such beauty if our happiness was not His intention? See the beauty so often taken for granted in the laugh of a loved one, in the touch of a child's hand, in the sweet perfection of a flower, and in all the small daily occurrences intended to bring pleasure.

Happiness and unhappiness comes from within. It is perception that determines judgment—the good or bad of a situation—the lovelessness or love-potential of a situation. It is whether we see a flower or a weed. It is how we perceive ourselves that determines our self-worth.

Unhappiness is a residual from the past that hangs on to influence our present and future. It is love withheld in the past and the love we deny ourselves in the present. Unhappiness creates negativity in our actions and reactions, negativity in how we perceive ourselves, others, and the world.

So, be happy.

NOW LET'S GO IN PEACE TO LOVE AND SERVE THE LORD AND EACH OTHER!

About This Book

Addiction is no longer limited to drug and alcohol abuse. It has expanded in American society to include almost all human activities that can be performed in excess. Excess seems to be today's standard as we strive for the bigger, the better, the more.

We need things to replace what is missing from our lives. Things to disguise who and what we are.

So, who and what are we? What is missing from our lives? *Addictive Lies* attempts to answer these questions by incorporating Christian fundamentals into psychological thought. It presents a God-based view of addiction, determining the cause and providing practical suggestions for a cure.

Dr. VM Lawrence is a graduate of several major Pennsylvania universities in addition to religious certification programs. Having worked in a variety of educational and private mental health facilities, her experience with addiction is both personal and professional.

Addictive Lies is the culmination of years of self-discovery as she questioned and battled addiction until God's truth finally materialized. It is God's truth that saves us from addiction. And this truth is too good not to share.

For comments and/or to contact author please visit Addictivelies.com.